LIONS
IN THE
GRASS

LIONS
IN THE
GRASS

A Marketing Insider's Guide to MASS PERSUASION

(and why you want the Sh!t you want)

BILL MORRISON

LIONS IN THE GRASS

A Marketing Insider's Guide to Mass Persuasion
(and why you want the Sh!t you want)
BILL MORRISON

Published by Newterra Publishing
Copyright © 2020 by Bill Morrison
First Edition

PAPERBACK ISBN 978-1-7773101-1-0
HARDCOVER ISBN 978-1-7773101-0-3
EBOOK ISBN 978-1-7773101-2-7

COVER & TEXT DESIGN Jazmin Welch
EDITOR Lori Bamber
PUBLISHING SUPPORT TSPA The Self Publishing Agency Inc.

To Tanya, Will and Finn
My three reasons

CONTENTS

PREFACE

IN THE 1996 MOVIE *THE GHOST AND THE DARKNESS*, Val Kilmer plays an engineer sent to East Africa to complete an ill-fated railway project. The bridge construction is easy—the challenge is the two lions hunting the work camp, named the Ghost and the Darkness by local tribespeople. Day and night, the lions appear from nowhere to stalk and attack terrified workers, wreaking emotional and psychological havoc. The men soon realize that to fight back and survive, they must understand how these lions think.

Today, for most of us, lions are just an old dream lodged deep in our DNA. But their patience and power still surround us in the marketers, advertisers, product designers, PR professionals and influencers who are paid to manipulate us. They are emotional exploiters, highly skilled at convincing and controlling. They control what you click on social media, decide elections, determine what you buy and when, and how much you're willing to pay. The only way to outwit them—the only way to be free—is to understand what they do and why.

Welcome to the dark art of emotional manipulation. Here you will learn the techniques, tactics and secrets of emotional influence and control of others—so you can be a little more lion and a little less dinner.

About 900 people waited in line for a chance to buy one of the 300 condominiums I was selling. Most arrived before dawn, waiting anxiously for the sales center to open. At noon sharp, the doors swung wide and the room filled to capacity. Buyers poured in. Scrambling, screaming and pleading—demanding to know if their suite choices were available.

Crushed against the back wall by this human tide, I fought to update the massive availability board. With every SOLD sticker I placed, the crowd's anxiety grew more intense. Demand eclipsed availability. Fear of loss replaced rational thinking; competition eliminated common sense. Buyers grabbed anything they could, sensing that in a few hours every home would be sold. They were right.

Chaos.

Unable to find a salesperson, a woman in red fought her way through the crowd and grabbed my jacket.

"Give me four condos," she yelled, pointing at the big board.

"Four?" I repeated.

"Yes, four. I don't care which ones," she said. "All these people can't be wrong."

INTRODUCTION

OVER THE YEARS, I've been called a few things. A manipulative bastard, a mad marketing scientist, "a user of persuasive tricks and tactics to sell out my high-rise towers," and a real asshole (for running out of hot dogs on opening sales day).

This tapestry of unflattering monikers is, in a way, a badge of honor. While I don't like being called anything derogatory, I do know that when you create demand that far exceeds supply, there are bound to be a few, ahem, upset folks.

For longer than I care to remember, I've been marketing, selling and lining people up to buy presale condominiums in multifamily developments. To do so, I committed early to constantly experimenting with emotional influence.

Each of these experiments has been conducted in real-life situations over the past 30 years. While some were incredibly successful, others were embarrassing failures. Yet they all shared something in common—each provided unparalleled insight into human behavior and decision processes. Uncovering the patterns behind what motivates our actions was ultimately far more valuable than any particular outcome.

These results provided the framework for an astonishingly effective persuasion model, one that consistently connects with an audience emotionally, drives actions and influences decisions. (I've also learned that when you sell all your condos on opening day, you'd better have enough hot dogs. Really.)

Upon finishing this book, you'll understand why we human folk choose one brand over its competitors. You will know why we feel good spending money in some retail environments yet can't wait to escape others, why one advertisement makes us hit "add to cart" while others make us press the escape button, and why some presentations bring an audience to their feet and others put them to sleep.

You'll learn why a once-loved brand is no longer coveted and understand your desire to exchange an object at precisely the same time the new model is introduced. You'll know why we pay more at an auction than at a store for the same product, and why we're happy to do it. You will realize why negative headlines draw us in while we don't bother to read past positive ones, and why people in crowds think and act differently than when they're alone—and how this is all based on evolution.

When you've turned the last page, you will understand which outside influences affect your decisions and, just as significantly, know why and how others reach theirs.

When you finish this book, you will recognize what leads, controls, influences and manipulates your behavior. You'll understand the power of emotional persuasion.

You'll also know how to use it.

In short, you'll have all the tools and techniques of the professional persuaders and will be fully capable of wielding them to achieve the results you want in every aspect of your business and personal life.

Most importantly, you will become a true emotional revolutionary.

Now, on with the persuading. Because, as the lady in red said:

"All these people can't be wrong."

THE DARK ART OF EMOTIONAL MANIPULATION

MARKETERS, PERSUADERS AND ADVERTISERS infiltrate every surface, crack and crevasse of our already slender attention span.

The attack is relentless. Driven hard by an age-old monetary motivation, they have one objective: To sell their sh!t.

In response to this battering, we've become selective and more elusive. We evade television commercials with PVRs and rub the lettering off the fast-forward button on our remote controls. We dismiss print advertising as fast as pages can turn and hover our cursors over the "SKIP AD" button, anxiously watching the five-second countdown that keeps us from our YouTube download.

Signage is ignored; radio advertising slides off us like eggs from Teflon.

To survive, we've become extremely attention selective. Impatient and intolerant. This is natural. It is evolution.

As our avoidance of the persuader's efforts intensifies, we humans have become, as the marketers quip, "disturbingly difficult to reach."

Some marketers try harder, with more advertising in more places. But this only increases the noise, driving us further away. While others don't try harder, they get darker. They get emotional.

PROFESSIONAL PERSUADERS—of whom I am one—are increasingly turning to the dark arts of emotional manipulation.

Rather than positioning ads and messages out front for all to see, persuaders are the new lions in the grass. Stalking the subconscious, pouncing on emotion and outwitting ever-evolving human defenses.

It's an effective approach because it is undetected. Most people believe that emotion plays a small part in their decision-making process and that the power of persuaders and influencers is modest at best. When asked, they'll say their decisions are made after careful, logical consideration of the facts. In truth, the more logical we believe we are, the more susceptible to manipulation we become.

As we move through these pages together, I'll discuss how this misconception is at the core of every persuader's influence.

Knowledge is a powerful defense against the persuader's Machiavellian maneuvers, but this isn't just something you need to be aware of. In today's world of overwhelming attention demand, you need to know how to use the dark art of persuasion to be heard above the noise and survive.

It's no longer enough to make your pitch for a raise or presentation logically sound. Every market is saturated with sleepy offerings boasting "Great Value!" that get scrolled past or end up at the bottom of the compost pail.

To be effective today, you need to know the combination of techniques that influence behavior. It is the difference between creating desire and disinterest. To achieve this, you don't have to know how your audience thinks, but you do have to know how they feel.

With this understanding, you will become an effective persuader.

Interested? I hope so.

But before we get started, a word about "manipulation." When used in regard to relationships between humans, the most common definition is something like this one, provided by the Merriam Webster Dictionary.

: to control or play upon by artful, unfair, or insidious means, especially to one's own advantage

Nobody really likes the word manipulate. It's associated with immorality, such as trickery, lies and deceit.

For some, just hearing the expression causes an emotional reaction. It makes us want to rise up and defend our free will against its forces.

I'm not about to challenge the pedigree, history or foundation of the word. Nope, I agree, "manipulate" is associated with some pretty unscrupulous intentions.

But what I do like is that, all on its own, the word triggers an emotional reaction, and that is exactly what this book is about.

While you have every right to judge the word, I'm going to ask that, for the next few hundred pages of your time, you temporarily consider it just a word that describes a process.

I ask this of you because I need to employ it with freedom and use it to express both good and evil—to present how best to wield its power and avoid its control.

Now, as Julia Long started her 1950s BBC Radio program: "Are you sitting comfortably? Then I will begin …"

To manipulate, of course—but for your own good.

WHY I WROTE THIS BOOK AND
WHY IT SHOULD MATTER TO YOU

BUYING: A TOPIC THAT WAS PROBABLY NOT DISCUSSED on the steps of the Pantheon. Too bad, really. Because deep thinking on the parallels of buying and selling would have been genuinely helpful. After all, everyone buys, and everyone sells.

Selling includes asking your boss for a raise, convincing your kids to eat broccoli, pitching investors, peddling school fundraising chocolates, supporting political candidates, and convincing spouses, co-workers, friends and family members of the merits of your ideas.

Marketing and selling everything in this universe, from hockey sticks to your trustworthiness, requires that you convince your audience.

Because we buy stuff every day, we **think** we are good at buying and believe that our choices are under our control. We have faith that our decisions are the result of fact-gathering and logic.

But this isn't the case. At all.

In almost every situation, our decisions are manipulated by our own emotions. Independent thought and logic are disregarded. (Until after the decision is made, but more on that later.)

» "I'm not buying that car; something about how it looks bothers me."
Emotion or logic?
» "I'm not voting for that candidate; she seems untrustworthy."
Emotion or logic?
» "I don't know what it is, but I just like shopping here!"
Emotion or logic?

» "Everyone is buying; I have to get one before prices go up."
Emotion or logic?

Most decisions are emotional and externally influenced, but most individuals believe their choices are made through careful consideration and reached independently.

Nothing could be further from the truth.

Once our decision has been made, we subconsciously create strong fact-based validations for our original (emotional) decision. We reengineer our consideration process. Like it or not, we fool ourselves. In doing so, we mislead ourselves about our motivation. We help the manipulators manipulate.

This practice of adjusting the truth about our purchase decisions is especially harmful when we try to sell or persuade someone. First, we convince ourselves that we make decisions differently than we do, and then we believe other people do the same. You can foresee the results.

IN THE MOVIE *A FEW GOOD MEN*, Tom Cruz plays a military lawyer, Daniel Kaffee. In the courtroom drama, he cross-examines Jack Nicholson's character, Colonel Jessup. The movie's most famous scene comes when Kaffee demands to know if Jessup doctored the flight logbooks, changing the details after the fact to hide the truth and better suit his needs.

Colonel Jessup: You want *answers*?!

Kaffee: *I want the truth!!!*

Colonel Jessup: *YOU CAN'T HANDLE THE TRUTH!!!*

Like Colonel Jessup's logbooks, our decision-making processes are altered after the fact, and we cover emotion's tracks with rationale. Once the heart is satisfied with an emotional choice, we justify our decision with logic, and emotion's part in the process is eliminated in our consciousness.

Consider your own rationale.

If you're part of a married couple, chances are at least one of you is wearing a diamond. Statistically, in Western culture, about eight out of 10 female spouses sport this small pricey rock.

The decision to spend any money at all, let alone the well-publicized "three months' salary," when a simple band would do can't be based on logic. Can it?

Before the 1950s, few people proposed with diamonds. It was the collective efforts of De Beers Consolidated Mines and Philadelphia ad agency N.W. Ayer & Son that changed the public's perception of diamonds as jewelry for the rich. Suddenly they were proof of eternal commitment for everyone.

Whether or not we long for diamonds or the means to put a carat or two on our beloved's finger, at some level we connect the emotion of love with the very unemotional lump of compressed carbon.

It's been over 70 years since the first ads proposed, "A Diamond is Forever," yet emotion still dictates our behavior. But to cover up emotion's control, our mind rationalizes the purchase as an investment based on carats, clarity, setting, price and brand. Rationale steps in, and we tell ourselves this is what people do. Without a diamond, I could look cheap, unromantic or even unloving. What kind of fool would propose without a diamond?

Emotion calls the shots—and rationale takes the credit. Or, emotion is the stick, while rationale concentrates on the carats.

Cognitive scientists call this process of self-delusion post-choice rationalization. Sigmund Freud, a founder of psychoanalysis, believed that our subconscious connects our emotions and our past experiences to who we are, strongly influencing our personality, behavior, and ultimately, our decisions.

Believing that logic is ultimately responsible for our decisions, we attempt to persuade in the same logical way. Consider the man who purchases a car because it makes him feel vibrant, sexy and alluring—but tries to sell it a few years later by highlighting its safety features, gas mileage and reliability.

I BUY, THEREFORE I AM (GOOD AT SELLING).

THIS MISPERCEPTION IS ULTIMATELY RESPONSIBLE for most presentation failures. Too often we sell based on how we **believe** we buy (logically) rather than how and why we **actually** buy (emotionally).

We try to convince others with features, facts and details.

Without emotion, our efforts to convince underwhelm. Using too much detail, we trigger a need to compare our view or product to others. (More on this later.) Ultimately, we just fail to connect.

To break these destructive patterns, we have to concede that our emotions drive our actions and decisions more than we want to admit and that our emotions are being manipulated by external influences—the persuaders.

There is light at the end of this tunnel. Those who understand how accessible, vulnerable and controllable an audience's emotions are will do well. Those who capitalize on this knowledge will do really, really well.

The purpose of this book is to identify the true nature of human decision-making, and show how it can be predicted and manipulated in order to:

1. Influence others
2. Understand and outwit the persuaders
3. Become an emotional revolutionary
4. All of the above

Through these pages, you will come to understand your own decisions and learn to wield these persuasive practices, becoming a true emotional revolutionary for the forces of good.

Let's start by understanding emotional irrationality.

"Dear marketers, I'm making a major purchase and wondered if you could manipulate my decision," said no one ever.

Earlier, I mentioned the lady in red who made a multimillion-dollar buying decision based on how everyone else was acting.

She could be considered irrational.

You could think of her as lacking logic or incapable of independent thought, being influenced by her environment, or as a victim of emotional manipulation. But that would likely be a case of the pot calling the kettle black while living in a glass house.

"I've always wanted a sit-down riding mower even though our yard is not huge. But—if I spent less time on the weekend cutting grass, I'd have more time with the kids. Buying this ride-a-mower is good for my family."

"No, I almost never leave the city—but this four-wheel drive off-road vehicle, complete with undercarriage skid plates, will be safer on the (three?) snow days we get in Vancouver. And at any moment, I COULD click a button inside my leather-appointed, $100,000 SUV and go bush-bashing to get away from it all."

This process of introspective illusion may help us feel better about our decisions, but it creates an inaccurate perception of our behavior. Redefining our actions as unemotional means we give our emotions little credit or protection.

It is the very fact that we consider our emotions so exclusively under our control that makes persuaders so dangerous. We fail to consider that, like a double agent, it's our own emotions that enable outsiders to manipulate our actions.

The reality is that access to our personal emotions can be achieved in seconds.

HELLO. MY NAME IS BILL.

I'M A MANIPULATOR.

And I'm sorry.

I've spent a lifetime manipulating emotions. Making people feel needy, angry, happy, sad, fulfilled, accepted, included, loved, rejected, vilified and anxious.

One way or another, I've slid past fortified human defenses, accessed my audience's emotions and created frenzied lineups of hair-pulling, fist-throwing, chair-tossing buyer madness. All of it by influencing the emotions of sound-minded, clear-thinking adults, who, when confronted with the correct stimuli, respond with irrational predictability.

I market presale condominiums (essentially, not-yet-built boxes of air). But it would be a mistake to consider this a real estate marketing book. These ideas are equally applicable in any industry or situation.

Regardless of the product, service or idea you're presenting, understanding how emotion influences action is the key to success.

Whether you want to control your market's buying decisions, change another person's mind, avoid being on the other end of a persuading puppeteer's strings or just want your kids to do more homework, it's critical to realize how our emotions are accessed and influenced.

This means understanding how and why emotions guide our behavior as well as knowing the techniques behind persuasion. Doing so enables us to avoid being at the mercy of the dark arts, and ultimately, to leverage these persuasion tactics for good.

You, dear reader, are not a logical person. You are emotional. And you are being controlled and influenced by professional persuaders, without your knowledge. Every. Single. Day.

How does that statement make you feel? Angry? Intrigued? Skeptical? Whatever it is, you feel something, and that's the point. It's important, because it's the first example of how unguarded our emotions actually are.

With just a few words, images or gestures, persuaders can slip behind our defenses. And once access is achieved, they're only steps away from using our own emotions to manipulate us any way they wish.

Throughout the years, this emotional espionage has become intensely effective at bypassing our defenses. It's moved from being largely unknown and experimental to finding its way into every aspect of our lives, and it's accelerating.

For me, the need to understand how to access my audience's emotions and manipulate their actions began at school.

Grade school.

"Never let schooling interfere with education."

Grant Allen, *Eyes and No Eyes*, 1894

CHAPTER 1

EMOTIONAL EDUCATION

I FINISHED GRADE 12 BELIEVING TWO THINGS—I was illiterate and I hadn't learned a thing. I was half right.

Mistaking my moderate dyslexia for low intelligence, I felt completely inadequate from an early age.

Certain letters and numbers appeared reversed and were unexplainably interchangeable. The other kids seemed to understand everything so easily. My only conceivable conclusion was that I was just stupid.

The teachers ascribed my poor results to a "lack of attentiveness" and a "failure to apply myself" and they set out to refocus my attention.

Nothing worked.

One teacher taped me to my desk, generating great laughter from the class but doing little to help with concentration. Another, believing more discipline was needed, often used the full swing of a yardstick to emphasize the point.

His motto, "Spare the Rod, Spoil the Child," was written front and center, above the blackboard. ***s9are the rob, s9oil the chilb***. It was the early 1970s, and while that teaching style was fading in popularity, it was still acceptable within the closed classroom.

Mr. Sullivan, if you read this, I'd love to discuss those days—perhaps in a closed classroom.

I spent my school days terrified that students and teachers would discover my stupidity. While my classmates studied, I focused on survival and finding ways to hide my embarrassing flaws.

I concentrated on what affected a classroom's behavior and learning how to change its energy and momentum. I studied how to respond to questions without answering. I discovered ways to deflect focus onto others and learned how to change a teacher's determination to fail me into belief that a passing grade was their best decision.

I learned conversational distractions and diversions, and to pull discussions away from anything that exposed my weaknesses by gently guiding focus to where I was less vulnerable.

I began to understand how similar language produced completely different responses if the presentation was changed only slightly. I started to appreciate the power of language, and how different approaches to the same subject influenced the audience's response.

I learned that emotion moved people in ways rationale could not. Reasoning with a teacher to change her mind on my grade had little impact—but asking about her own feelings of being back at school and connecting those emotions with my grades certainly did.

Along the way, I gathered the secrets of influence. I learned to survive by emotional maneuvering.

WHAT BEGAN AS ANXIETY AND FEAR manifested into an education in how people feel, behave and react.

I left school completely illiterate, but I didn't leave uneducated. I eventually turned my experience in human behavior into a successful marketing career. Along the way, I've come to understand that the product doesn't matter, nor does the market's condition. If you access your audience's emotions, you can connect people to your product, service or offering and generate incredible demand.

The foundation of persuasion is understanding that emotion is connected to our experiences and memory.

EMOTIONAL EXCAVATION

YEARS AGO, MY GRANDMOTHER PASSED AWAY. Her unconditional love and complete acceptance of me remain among my most pleasant memories.

When my father exchanged his house-based existence for one of adventure, he cleared out the family home of everything that wouldn't fit on a sailboat bound for Mexico. He offered me my grandmother's collectables.

I loved her very much, but at 19 years of age, the thought of owning ceramic garden gnomes wasn't appealing, and my contesting their delivery created a brief but vibrant discussion on the value of memory.

However terrible a person the refusal of Grandma's hand-painted gnomes makes me, I assure you that my rejection of the ceramics in no way makes my memories of her any less important. I simply didn't connect with them, and I realized that displaying garden gnomes would have dramatically reduced my chances of ever landing a girlfriend.

In emotional contrast to this is my grandfather's Freemason ring. It was the only jewelry he wore, and I grew up looking at that ring on his huge hands, then down at my own, wondering if they would ever grow.

My grandfather communicated with his hands, tussled my hair and patted my shoulders. Tales were told of his strength and toughness. Granddad let his hands do the talking, and they said all that was needed.

For me, his old silver ring with its tarnished brass inlay was fascinating. When he passed, it meant everything that he left it to me.

I loved both my grandparents equally, but with the same effort I sought ownership of the ring (pardon the Hobbit reference) I avoided stewardship of the gnomes. To me, the ring held sweet memories of my grandfather; the gnomes reminded me only of 1950s suburbia.

Like the difference between Granddad's ring and Grandma's ceramics, the significance of an object is determined not by the value it gives us but by the value we give it. Ultimately, the level of our *emotional connection* to something determines our desire to acquire it and the degree to which we value it.

IT'S HOW WE BOND WITH BRANDS, sports teams, lawnmowers and SUVs. Once we recognize what we want, we connect with it and form our almost unbreakable emotional bond with these emotionless objects.

But what initially influences us to seek out this connection? How did it evolve to have such a deep emotional hold?

If we look back at our strongest connections to preferred products, brands, objects or beliefs, it very often had little to do with the actual object and much to do with the emotion it created.

So why do we want one thing more than another based on an emotional connection? Is our loyalty misguided? Is our common sense mistaken? Brand lovers swear their selection is logic based on quality and preference, but taste tests constantly surprise participants when packaging is hidden. Could it be that our preferences are dictated by forces beyond our conscious level? To answer this, it's best we look inwards, and backwards.

A song can bring us right back to a precious moment in our history. A crisp white sheet hanging on a clothesline can conjure up our eight-year-old self, riding a bike in the backyard. Human beings are walking storage vaults of emotion-laden memories, all of them eagerly awaiting retrieval—by us, or by someone else.

SAFECRACKING THE EMOTIONAL VAULT

THE VOLUME OF UNIQUE MEMORIES in our personal storage vault is staggering. Especially considering we gather new memories, consciously and subconsciously, every passing second as we encounter new environments and experiences. Add to this our pre-stocked instincts (the ones we inherit in our DNA) and it's clear our vaults are packed full, all of it just waiting for recollection.

While the content of these vaults is predominately personal and exclusively our own, what isn't unique is the way we store and access it.

It's this storage and retrieval process that enables outsiders to manipulate our behavior, and the best persuaders know it.

Believing our emotions are inaccessible by outsiders only compounds the issue. It's as if we've locked the doors to our emotional storage vaults and proudly consider them impenetrable—while all of humanity's locks share the same combination.

Professional persuaders understand that emotion is the combination that unlocks their audience's vault—and once inside they have complete control over our behavior.

Be it creating dramatic demand for your product, avoiding professional persuasion or convincing your kids to do their chores, understanding the role of emotions in the decision process gives you an incredible life advantage.

Learning the persuader's techniques is the first step but, up first, a little emotional espionage …

CHAPTER 2

EMOTIONAL ESPIONAGE
THE DARK ART

KRYSTYNA SKARBEK WAS CROWNED MISS POLAND AT JUST 17. A few years later, she was in the British Intelligence Service, a subversion agent and espionage expert working against the Nazis.

What makes her incredibly interesting in the context of persuasion is the ease with which she repeatedly moved past German defenses and used emotional espionage to operate behind enemy lines.

During World War II, her most challenging mission was to free fellow spies on the eve of their execution in German-occupied France.

Using fear, reward and other emotional tactics, Krystyna manipulated the prison's commanding officer into believing the Allied forces were on the verge of taking the city and would soon have him in captivity.

She convinced the officer that the local citizens hated him, and the Allied Forces intended to turn him over to the blood-hungry French mob.

Skarbek orchestrated the freedom of her colleagues by using emotion to persuade the officer that liberating the prisoners would earn him favor, freedom and financial reward from the Allies. (Rather than being torn limb from limb by the French.)

The commanding officer's emotion overpowered his common sense. Skarbek persuaded him to release the prisoners and escape with them back to the Allies—where I'm sure he was surprised when favor and fortune weren't actually what awaited him.

Working undetected behind enemy lines to influence and manipulate an outcome is espionage—using your audience's own fear, guilt and greed to manipulate their belief is emotional espionage.

ESPIONAGE. It's been around for a while. Wikipedia describes it as obtaining secret or confidential information without the owner's knowledge or permission.

It may seem easier to parachute in behind a hostile enemy's defenses than to access someone else's private and protected emotions, but the mind is not the impenetrable fortress it appears to be. Access is simple, because we have left the door unguarded—and it's been unguarded for millions of years.

We know what tugs at our heartstrings, but believe our choices are ultimately our own, determined by analytical review of facts and options.

We're wrong. This tragic inaccuracy about emotional espionage's substantial power has filled storage lockers with forgotten items and emptied bank accounts around the world.

This misreading of who and what is actually controlling our decision process allows the persuaders, those lions in the grass, to silently sidestep our common sense and take over the controls of our decision-making. It's a fact—or should I say an emotion—that's hard to accept. After all, no thinking person wants to acknowledge they are driven by outside influence. We carry on believing that our experiences, both earned and learned, guide our path. In doing so, we become easy prey.

How is this possible?

In an effort to understand and prepare for each new situation we may encounter, our minds work on multiple levels, continuously gathering, sorting and storing information, consciously and subconsciously.

Our conscious mind deals in facts, data and information retrieval, while our subconscious collects emotions, all to be stockpiled in our library-like memory.

It is an enormous amount of detail to be indexed and catalogued in a format that allows for immediate retrieval, and our subconscious does it by connecting each of our experiences to an emotion.

While our conscious mind takes credit for adding to this impressive experiential library, the subconscious is busy acting as librarian, categorizing our experiences according to the powerful emotions to which they're attached.

Think of your earliest memories. The details, like looking through the wavy glass of an old window, are blurry and undefined. But the emotions attached to those memories are rarely out of focus. Consider again the white sheet billowing on a clothesline or a favorite song that transports you back in time—the feelings we had are so easily remembered.

Persuaders understand that the core of decision-making is emotion (the heart) not rational thinking (the head). They know that to influence an audience's thinking, the message must be precise, yet to influence emotion they only need to be close, and empathy will do the rest.

When we're faced with a new emotional experience, environment or situation, our minds immediately search our personal storage vaults for a relatable emotion to improve our understanding of the experience.

It isn't that we humans are overly emotional. It's that we have an insatiable need to relate. Persuaders know that access to an audience's emotional storage is best accomplished by evoking empathy. Because we store our memories with connected emotions, if persuaders present a relevant emotion, even a general one, it triggers our instinctive search for the appropriate reaction. In this case, Empathy.

EMOTIONAL EMPATHY

FOR EMPATHY TO BE TRIGGERED, the emotion evoked doesn't need to be identical. If you've never won a state championship or lost a pet, it's difficult to relate to that exact experience, but we can still relate with the emotions of joy or sadness in our own emotional storage vault.

The better our minds are at generating empathy, the more likely we are to create stronger personal connections. In evolutionary terms, this correlates directly with survival. Evolutionary success is tilted toward humans quick to understand new experiences by relating them to their past, and to those able to build relationships by expressing empathy toward others.

Even though we no longer cohabitate with dire wolves and saber-tooths, we are still evolutionarily programmed to behave as if our survival is *always* at stake and relating to others remains at the top of our survival instincts.

With almost eight billion people on our crowded planet, the need to relate is constant. This makes empathy a critical tool. And when we need to relate emotionally, we can't waste time searching our vault's endless files. So, we go directly to the section with the relevant emotion so we can accurately understand and predict how to act in every situation.

This refined search process allows for immediate retrieval. But there's a trade-off: it offers little time to question information's validity, or the presenter's true purpose.

This is our Achilles' heel, something persuaders rely upon.

So when a soap commercial about self-consciousness and inner beauty interrupts our regularly scheduled TV program, we can't help but unconsciously search our storage for relatable emotions.

Our unconscious predisposition to empathize is what makes emotional marketing (when done correctly) so powerful.

FEATURES VERSUS EMOTIONS

YET SOME WOULD-BE MARKERS STILL DISMISS EMOTION'S ROLE.

Even large corporations fall victim to introspective illusion.

"Each box contains two scoops of raisins!"
"Each of our bars of soap has three ounces of moisturizer."
"Probably the best lager in the world."
"The new class of world class."
"Weekday Eggs cook faster than regular eggs." (Wait, they what…?)

If you recognize any of these slogans, it's because of their expensive exposure. By relying on years of repetition, these companies become vulnerable to competitors doing one simple thing, using emotional connection, something we'll discuss later in detail.

For now, it's sufficient to say that this miscalculation results in massive marketing budgets. It's an expensive mistake. Given enough budget, it's possible to carpet-bomb any audience into submission. That is, until budgets shrink or someone else advertises three scoops of raisins in their flakes or four ounces of moisturizer in their soap or six blades in their razor. Then what?

WHEN COMPARED TO CONSUMER LOYALTY built on an emotional connection, campaigns presenting facts and features fail to hold their audience—or worse, encourage them to go away.

Without the power of emotion, campaigns underwhelm. But this is the least of your marketing or persuasion worries! Focusing on features and details actually creates a reaction opposite to the one desired. It triggers the human need to compare, and that is a journey from which many never return.

THE HIGH COST OF DETAIL

EVOLUTION HAS SEEN TO IT THAT HUMANS ARE HARDWIRED with a great many instincts and abilities. But we didn't evolve with the ability to assess value except through comparison. Descriptive detail has no bearing on value unless it can be evaluated against similar detail. Are Samsung refrigerators with FlexZone technology better than LG fridges with LoDecibel Operation? How do you know?

To persuade successfully, you must connect on an emotional level—and avoid presenting primarily based on features.

Can it really be that simple? Can you really roll out emotion that connects your offering with your audience? Can you really leverage emotion to do the heavy lifting, deliver your message and influence your audience's action?

Yes.

And it starts by mastering the art of emotional *story-selling*.

"To survive, you must tell stories."

Umberto Eco

CHAPTER 3

ANCIENT TECHNOLOGY AND YOUR AUDIENCE'S EMOTIONS

SEATED IN A CROWD OF 15,000 somehow tucked into the Vegas auditorium, I waited patiently for the keynote speaker. She was the dean of a large university and the author of several books. I was excited to hear her insights.

The emcee was late-night talk show host Jay Leno. A natural, he warmed up the crowd with his signature combination of humor and entertainment, polished by many years in the business.

The keynote speaker appeared as Leno completed his introduction.

She seemed hesitant, nervous, unsure of where to begin. Her voice was weak and timid. It must have been tough to follow a seasoned entertainment veteran, and the stress was showing. It took a minute, but she pulled it together and started into her presentation.

The event was an international real estate convention and I was there as a guest of a conference sponsor. My role was to watch, listen and provide feedback on their participation. A great gig—go to Vegas, take it all in and comment. In Las Vegas, there's no shortage of material to comment on!

The crowd was generous and forgave her nervous start. But as her presentation continued, the energy in the room changed. Empathy turned to apathy. Disinterest gained momentum and the crowd grew uncomfortable. A few people stood up to leave and soon the aisles flooded with an exodus to the exit doors.

Her credibility was well earned, her topic well researched, and her content appropriate to the audience. But the seats continued to empty. It was a statement she had to hear loud and clear.

She told stories, but they were third-party examples, related to our industry but unrelated to her. Without connecting the stories to her own life, she couldn't connect them to ours. Soon thousands of people began to leave.

She ended her presentation, scheduled for an hour, after only 25 minutes. I'm sure the embarrassment of seeing people head for the exit took its toll. She thanked those of us still in our seats and turned to walk off the stage.

Then something strange happened. Jay Leno walked out, shook her hand—and didn't let it go.

His grip seemed to tighten as she tried to exit the stage. Her eyes wide with surprise, her body facing the exit, feet moving, her entire body wanted off that stage. Still Leno held his ground and kept her in front of the audience.

Hands grasped, they remained connected as Leno asked a question, then another, and another, as he gently guided her back to the middle of the stage.

Of the anecdotes she used in her speech, he asked questions such as, "And how did that make you feel?" "What do you think about that situation?" and "What's your take on this?"

Mesmerized, I hardly noticed that people had stopped heading to the exits. Now people began to sit down again and listen—not to Leno's queries but to the speaker's personal connection with each story.

When it became personal, it became emotional. It became relevant. Answering each question from her point of view, she revisited her speech and discussed the impact each element had on her personally. She began to connect with everyone in the crowd and we began to relate to her.

That day I realized the full power of emotion-connected story-telling— and just how cool Jay Leno really is!

Good storytelling is like good story-selling. It's effective emotional espionage. It tiptoes past an audience's defenses to connect and influence at a deep, undetected level.

Is story-selling powerful enough to connect to your audience's emotion *and* intensify their desire to act? Can it get them to pay more attention (and more money) than a good old commonsense presentation of facts and details?

Yep. And the best-selling brands know it.

These brands use emotion to sell their story, not sell their product.

"Have a Coke and a smile."

"Just do it."

"There are some things that money can't buy. For everything else, there's MasterCard."

More than catch phrases, this is language that emotionally connects us to a brand through its story.

The intention of all great advertising is to move people rather than try to sell product. Stories move us because they are exponentially more powerful than facts. It's how we communicate as a species; it's what we've evolved to pay attention to. It is what we need.

DETAILS VERSUS EMOTIONS IN STORY-SELLING

"LION!"

"Where's the lion? Is it sleeping? What is it doing? Did it chase you? Were you scared?"

Come on, give me the story!

Storytelling is natural. It's instinctual. It's how we communicate when we're at our best. Presenting stories is deep in our DNA. We've survived and flourished because we've told stories.

Stories connect us to other humans—story-selling is the same.

It's why a television commercial can connect us to a product through their stories about a caring parent's love for a child and do it in less than 30 seconds.

This works because we process emotional stories in the way we process actual experiences, meaning we retain emotionally relevant presentations and stories much more easily. It's the difference between remembering a professor's lecture and our first kiss. Emotions we remember. Facts we forget.

Given the ever-increasing volume of marketing we are forced to consume, stories have become the calm within the storm. They are the way brands can communicate above the noise. And when stories are shared with emotion and relevance, they are highly influential.

Let's say it is your executive assistant's birthday. People in the office are off to buy flowers. Not you. You want to do something better, be a little different. Entering the gift shop, you're overloaded with options. This is a work relationship, so the gift needs to be professional, yet with a personal touch that says, "I think you are doing a fantastic job and I really appreciate you."

There are so many choices. An entrance mat that says, "Shut the Front Door," a wallet shaped like bacon, a print of a cat in a Mona Lisa pose. Then you see the candle section. This reminds you how much she loves candles. Bingo!

The shelves are packed with candles, but nothing stands out. Then you spot the perfect style. They are unique in shape, color and texture—and they have a story.

You grab the first beeswax candle. Its description, attached by hemp twine, is handwritten on parchment paper.

"This beeswax is harvested by Tibetan monks who pollinate a harmonious blend of rare flowers. Planted beside the hives, the blossoms give these candles their unique floral fragrance. Wax is taken from the combs only once every three years and burns more sweetly than any other on earth. First created in their monastery more than two centuries ago, these candles have been used as the only light in the monks' rooms during their journey of self-discovery ever since."

The description ends with a blessing from the monks themselves:

"May this candle illuminate your own journey of self-discovery."

There are only two of these candles left, one with the handwritten parchment attached, for $32, and one missing the tag at the end of the twine, priced at $16.

Which do you buy?

When presented with this scenario, most say they would take both to the counter and ask if another tag was available. Upon hearing "no," they would purchase the more expensive candle with the parchment note attached.

This example illustrates the way that emotion—projected through story-selling, connected to the product, and ultimately transferred to the purchaser—amplifies perceived value.

The easiest way to sell anything to anyone at any time is by connecting your product, service or message to the personal emotions of your audience.

Again, you don't have to mirror your audience's exact feelings, but the more relevant you are, the better the result.

More and more companies are replacing their features-based approach with this kind of emotion-based marketing. When done right, the results are powerful.

Consider your own experience. Sitting alone at home, watching a half-hour television show on evaluating antiques, and suddenly you have tears on your cheeks—because of a commercial?!

A few days later, the commercial catches you again. Even though you recognize its trickery and remember how it ends, the ad still delivers a strong emotional impact.

How can a 30-second interruption in the middle of a program on a completely unrelated topic pack this kind of emotional dynamite? It should be impossible, yet there we are in our favorite chair, with our emotions hijacked by a soap commercial presenting a story about *the inner beauty in all of us.*

Dove's 2007 "Campaign for Real Beauty" elevated them from a well-known soap brand to a cultural conversation. They did it by sneaking past our well-trained defenses and connecting their brand with our emotions.

Dove abandoned their earlier fact-based approach, explaining how much moisturizer was included in each bar of soap, and instead focused on story-selling.

Emotional hijacking isn't new. This subtle dark art of persuasion has been used as far back as Aristotle. And while it is an incredibly effective way to connect a product to your audience, it remains a rarely used weapon in most marketing arsenals. (Politics and social media? That's another story, one we'll discuss later in the book.)

No matter how impressive, you can't use details to outperform an emotional campaign.

"Hey, buy our soap; it contains jojoba oil!" versus "Women everywhere understand the value of inner beauty." No contest.

If inner beauty isn't aligned with your emotions, don't worry, you're not their target audience. But how about puppies?

In their recent dog food commercials, Iams "A Boy and His Dog (named) Duck" campaign opens with a small boy feeding his puppy Iams dog food and continues with heart-tugging imagery of the two growing older together. It's the story of a lifelong love between a boy and his dog. For pet owners, Iams' target audience, the story may be an emotional broad stroke—you may be a middle-aged single white woman with a mixed-breed rescue dog or an interracial family with a purebred poodle—but the campaign still connects the brand on an emotional level that the detail-wielding competition can't achieve.

Not a pet person? Procter & Gamble is pretty sure that you're either a parent or a child of a parent. They pluck at your heartstrings with their campaign, "Pick Them Back Up." Their advertising presents the emotional story of moms supporting their kids from childhood spills to Olympic podiums. Mom was there at every stage of the journey and in the end the kids won gold and never forgot her love and support. Here's to you, moms. Now go buy our soap.

The campaign is aimed straight at the emotions of P&G's target audience. What parent doesn't support their child's dreams? What adult didn't have parents there to pick them back up, or dream of having those parents? It's a specific story that generates empathy because it relates to the emotions of a wide audience. Even if your child didn't step onto a soccer field, never mind an Olympic podium, the story still connects.

Emotional story-selling connects a brand's message with an audience's emotions. It evokes the human need to understand, empathize and relate through our own personal experiences.

Persuaders know that if it's relevant and emotional, a message will speak to a vastly diverse audience because it hits everyone in the exact same spot—the heart. Not the head.

The Institute of Practitioners in Advertising (IPA) found that marketing embedded with emotion performed nearly twice as well as campaigns based on rationale and facts.

The marketing folks who understand this power are trying new ways to make their quest for consumers less about differentiating features and more about distinguishing their brand through emotional connection.

Some, like Red Bull, substitute traditional advertising for brand positioning by connecting the product with the emotion of big visual spectacles. Logos on the helmet of a daredevil freefalling from the edge of space let the event's magnitude define its brand and connect it to their audience. (If we bought with logic, we might question the necessity of a helmet when plummeting to earth from the stratosphere, other than as, say, a logo-holder.)

Even if you've never leapt from a helium balloon 24 miles above the earth or jumped from a perfectly good airplane dressed in a Liberace-styled flying-squirrel suit, you most certainly have been up high enough to experience the fear of heights.

Who knows—perhaps you may be feeling some of that sensation right now, just thinking about it?

Tapping into an audience's library of emotional experiences is how Red Bull connects its brand to the combination of extreme excitement, fear and heroism that we associate with the word "thrilling."

It is the kind of differentiation that fact-based presentations simply can't achieve. Can you imagine a Red Bull spokesperson holding a can and describing its sucrose, glucose and caffeine content? Their market share would plummet faster than a Red Bull Speedo-clad cliff diver.

Some persuaders understand this power. Others refuse to evolve and continue to market their product features.

I get it. We all want to believe facts have more impact than feelings and that logic overpowers emotion. But it simply doesn't work this way. Emotional marketing motivates action, while features evoke our need for more information and comparison.

Consider the ultimate sacrifice—what would you risk your life for, emotions or facts? It's a question the military knows the answer to.

"And dying in your beds many years from now, would you be willing to trade all the days from this day to that for one chance, just one chance to come back here and tell our enemies that they may take our lives, but they'll never take our freedom?"

William Wallace, The Battle of Stirling, Scotland 1297
(As presented by the kilt-clad Australian, Mel Gibson)

CHAPTER 4

EMOTION VERSUS DETAIL: ONE OF THESE THINGS MOTIVATES BETTER THAN THE OTHER

IN THE FIVE YEARS MY MARKETING COMPANY OCCUPIED the top of a four-story office building, we watched a steady turnover of the tenants below us. Except for one, the Canadian Army Recruiting Centre.

Our daily routine included a trek for lunch that took us past the street-level windows of the recruiting office's inviting interior.

The army recruiters, dressed head to toe in camouflage, seemed oddly exposed in their environment, a combination of administrative office and boutique hotel lobby.

We marveled at the flow of applicants streaming through their doors. Each was greeted with a firm handshake, then toured through the majestically uniformed mannequins, fully armed and poised for battle. The journey concluded comfortably, on modern leather sofas.

FOR KING AND COUNTRY

EACH OF THE NEW APPLICANTS was interviewing to risk their life for about $36,000 per year. We wondered what the draw could possibly be. Perhaps it was the age-old enticement of patriotism and meaning, fighting, as they say, for "king and country."

But—come on. Regardless of the cool uniforms, people shoot at you, like, on purpose.

In the halls, we'd bump into the recruiters and nod our hellos. They seemed like good guys. Polite and professional, just doing their jobs. I don't think they even knew what my industry was, but I knew theirs, and we were in the same business—persuasion.

Same business, different challenges.

All I had to do was motivate people to buy new condos. A relatively easy challenge, considering the rewards are historically and empirically promising.

For the army recruiters, marketing is different. They want young men and women to sign up, go to foreign countries and possibly shoot at someone, who would, invariably, be inclined to shoot back. All for about the same pay as a Starbucks shift manager, where the chances of enduring life-threatening situations are far less and the coffee is noticeably better.

One afternoon, waiting for the elevator beside a uniformed officer, our conversation moved from the basic polite greetings to marketing. He offered us a tour.

Their environment was spectacular. A marketer's dream. Mannequins in battle dress, adorned with the latest weaponry, were set amid historic black and white images of victorious battles and medaled solders. Stylish leather furniture added an elegant casualness that seemed to convey immortality.

"Look at this place! How could you not sign up?" I asked.

"Easy now—we don't just take anyone," the officer replied. "You have to apply. You can't walk in off the street. There's a test, an application and an interview process."

Incredible! They'd even created a sense of exclusivity. If you are lucky enough to make it through the interview, you have a chance of getting hired and risking life and limb.

I thought I was good at marketing—against this, I was but an infant.

When it comes to emotional persuasion, the military is good. Really good. Their visitor experiential pathing, their emotional presentation of pride, honor and loyalty, and the imbued sense of self-worth are incredible. Everything is perfect, not a mortar shell askew.

Granted, the military has been attracting people to their world a lot longer than I've been attracting condo buyers to mine. But it was still a humbling experience, one that made me consider my own approach to experiential environments. (More on that later.)

Now, before you send me heated emails on the importance of freedom and the sacred history of the military, I'll stop you, using the same language I sputtered when I sat down with Canada's top Military Reserve Force officer.

"I am not disrespecting the profession in the slightest. I am only asking how the recruiting is so effective despite well-documented historic consequences. Is it the emotional reward of fighting for king and country?" I asked naively.

The officer chuckled, "No, it's not *Pro rege et patria.*" (Besting me again, with his use of the official Latin.)

"It's not like it was," he continued. "We've had to change and adjust. There's an emotion that is bigger than 'for king and country.' Now it's about a common objective, a common cause. It's not about fighting for a leader or an individual, a king, president or prime minister. If we were at war, fighting for our country has relevance and its own emotional pull.

But when we're not, joining the military is about something deeper. It's not about fighting for someone; it's about fighting for everyone, and that includes our nation. But once you enlist, it becomes all about standing for your team, your group, your unit."

Sitting in the cramped back office, walls packed with heroic imagery, I began to understand the similarities in our approach. Despite the difference in our missions, we both marketed emotion.

We continued to talk about the core motivation behind military recruitment and he gifted me with one final, vital comment:

"Facts alone can't motivate. It's emotion that brings people to act."

I left the recruiting office with incredible clarity.

FACTS, FEATURES AND DATA HAVE LITTLE POWER when presented without emotion. The only action they summon is a quest for more facts, features and data. A comparative evaluation of options isn't what you want when asking your soldiers to charge an enemy, or for that matter, asking an audience to buy your product instead of the competitor's.

Our cognitive minds are information-seeking organs. When presented with detail, we are compelled to identify the comparables.

If you're looking for a house and the first one you see seems to be a good fit, would you stop searching? How would you know if it's good value?

Consider this scenario of detail versus emotion. Your realtor takes you through an open house. You really like the home but have yet to see others. At the open house, there are other people who seem interested, and your realtor says, "I know this is the first home we've seen, but there are buyers here who look interested. If you like it, we could write an offer now and get ahead of any competition."

How would you feel? What would you do?

Typically, the need for comparison drives people to look at other homes. But what if, after seeing other homes, you realize how great the first home was? Now you write that offer but lose to a competing bid.

A week later, you find a home that's almost as good. Seeing another group looking at it, would you write an offer immediately?

What if you did, but lost to competition again? By the third home tour, how long would you wait to make an offer on a home you liked? Would you write an offer immediately? Would you offer more than the asking price?

What if the buyers of the first home couldn't get financing and it came back on the market? How fast would you act? What price would you offer this time?

Now consider that entire scenario again. This time, there are no other interested parties, no competing offers and no pressure from other buyers. Would your offer change? Would you offer less?

The point: for most buyers, these different scenarios have a dramatic impact on their actions and the price they would pay. Yet the homes' value didn't actually change—the only change was the emotions connected to it.

Value is subjective. If you remove the influence of emotion, it is impossible to determine value without comparison.

Facts distract; emotions attract.

"Once upon a time," "in a land far, far away"—these opening sentences from our childhood books are signals to us to suspend our comparison curiosity so we can lie back and enjoy the story. Emotional presentations work the same way as we connect with the story and the storyteller.

Using *only* facts numbs emotion. Your audience is therefore only paying partial attention. The part of them that is most alive is checked out. Much like discussing bedroom cleanliness with your video-game-preoccupied teen, chances are your pitch will earn nothing more than a pacifying nod.

Some details, facts and features are necessary to educate an audience, but these should be lightly sprinkled between moments of emotional connection.

Imagine watching the tide as it makes its way up the beach. The kids play in the sand, chasing a beach ball as it bounces ahead in the breeze. What would it be like to end your evenings right here with a glass of wine—to plan the day while watching the sea from your deck, enjoying your morning coffee?

This is the life you and your family deserve. You've taken care of everyone. Now it's time to take care of you, too. This home is everything you've worked so hard for. Pure happiness, right?

It has the three bedrooms and two bathrooms you wanted. The kitchen is beautifully equipped and spacious enough for your entire family to gather.

Yes, it is slightly over the price range we discussed. But for this, I know you may want to dig a bit deeper—you, your family and the next generations will be grateful you decided to be bold and make this home yours. And it's perfect for entertaining your friends—I can't imagine what will go through their minds when they walk through your front door!

It all comes down to the fact that it's everything you ever wanted—and everything you deserve.

This language is an example of using emotion to frame the details. Further along in a presentation, features and facts can be added. But up front, it must be "once upon a time" if you want to end with "and they lived happily ever after."

WITHOUT EMOTION, OUR DRIVE TO COMPARE CONTINUES even beyond a purchase.

Let's say you just purchased a new TV. You bring it home and proudly mount it on the wall. Sitting back, you are amazed at its clarity and definition. The picture is perfect; the sound is amazing. Your wife loves it, and you've been elevated to hero status by the kids. It's a proud moment.

The next morning, sleepy-eyed from binge-watching an HBO series until 3 AM, you sit mindlessly flipping through the flyers that pack today's local paper.

Suddenly, your coffee splashes from its cup as you spot the exact TV you just purchased, advertised for significantly less at another store.

Now you can't bear to look at your TV. Even glancing in its direction reminds you how much you overpaid. You'll get over it—the playoffs and the "So You Think You Can Dance" finale start next week—but it hurts.

If we had an internal mechanism enabling us to compare happiness and fulfillment (including the fact that for once the kids thought we were cool) against the price we paid for the TV, we would be capable of including satisfaction in our perception of value.

But we're not built like that. We are wired to compare facts. It's evolution, once again. Like a beagle on a scent, we can't help but track down comparative information.

Consider the most basic example: a parent, a child and a hot stove.

Most adults have experienced touching something burning hot. It's now an emotional memory, stored for the purpose of instant recollection.

As their child moves toward a hot stove, the parent immediately recalls the danger from their own emotionally connected memory and voices a factual warning: "Don't touch the hot stove, it will burn your fingers!" All fact, no emotion. (No, freaking out doesn't make for an emotional connection.)

The parent grows agitated as the child disregards the warning and continues toward the stove.

Later, after calm has resumed, the parent tries to understand the child's actions and reviews their own ineffective presentation.

FACT: The stove is hot.

FACT: Touching the stove will burn their fingers.

FACT: Burnt fingers will hurt.

But facts don't motivate. Emotion does.

Even at this level, facts inspire comparison and create the need for additional understanding. The parent's plea doesn't translate as intended. Instead it creates the opposite effect—the child feels compelled to seek their own comparative experience.

Keeping Jr.'s fingers safe from harm or presenting your product's spectacular benefits and effectiveness relies on your ability to connect emotionally.

Science backs this up: Our brain's orbitofrontal cortex (OFC) is involved in our decision-making when we face the unfamiliar.

By searching for situational similarities, our OFC develops expectations based on our past experiences. When evaluating new situations, the OFC examines our responses in relevant experiences and judges these against its **forecasted outcome.**

If the new experience relates to a former experience, the OFC presents the probable outcome. If it's unrecognizable, the OFC searches for more comparables.

If you've burnt your fingers before, the OFC identifies the comparable experience and expected outcome—there is no need to touch a hot stove again just to re-experience the pain. In situations where personally stored comparables aren't available, our need to compare becomes a powerful force.

The best persuaders understand the OFC's significance and that our need to compare can only be extinguished by emotion.

HARNESSING EMOTION

WHEN ASKED, MANY PEOPLE ASSOCIATE THE WORD EMOTION with things like tears, sadness or weakness. Persuaders know that emotion influences everything, from happiness to anger, elation to frustration.

I began my real estate career selling new townhomes and condominiums. Having little experience, my sales approach was based only on what I knew about buying.

I believed I was a rational consumer, and that others would react, as I did, to straightforward, informative presentations.

I sold the way I thought I bought.

I discussed every detail, fact and feature. I even included my competitors' information in my presentations for absolute transparency and ease of comparison.

Potential buyers praised my approach as refreshingly informative. It was incredibly encouraging feedback—yet they continued to buy from my competition. When I asked why, they usually said something like, "I'm not sure. It just seemed like a better fit over there."

I could only conclude that these decisions were simply the result of poor judgment. After all, my product was clearly better in price, quality and location, and I'd provided all the evidence to support this.

Those were thin years!

In good markets, I sold a little more, in bad markets a little less. As time passed, my results improved slightly, but I was still being badly outsold.

Then on one Wednesday afternoon, everything changed.

Like most days, I unlocked the sales trailer and took up my spot inside one of two claustrophobic rooms. On the left was the closing office, on the right, the sales area, its blueprint table surrounded by floor plans, color boards, cabinet samples and a home location and availability map. Not much, but it was sophisticated for its time.

I opened a newspaper (probably to search the want ads) and settled in for the day. Our advertising ran on Saturdays, and most people came in on the weekend. For some unknown reason, Wednesdays were the slowest day—I often closed without seeing a single person.

A car door slammed. I dropped my paper. Customers!

I greeted the nice young couple as they entered my little sales area. I was just about to start describing our homes in detail when another customer walked in, a middle-aged man with a French-Canadian accent.

Three potential buyers, and on a Wednesday! This was incredibly unusual. I was about to start my presentation when the door opened once again, and another couple squeezed into the small space. They had been in weeks before, but I had no idea they were returning to buy a home—and I don't think they knew it either. Then, as if on cue, the man with the accent said, "This is where everyone is buying—it must be a good deal. I think I want two."

Then it got crazy.

My repeat visitors, sensing the urgency, snapped to attention and announced, "We are here to buy number 33."

Doing the best to hide my surprise, I showed them into the office area. Behind me I could hear the man from Quebec saying, "I knew it, these will be all gone in no time."

The first visitors leaned into the office. Panic had taken hold. "We want number 42," they said, then stepped back into the sales area loudly telling everyone, "42 is ours!"

The man from Quebec responded, "I knew it. Gone in no time!"

I'd finished the first contracts and begun talking to the couple wanting #42 when the door opened again!

It was a well-dressed man who announced that he only wanted a price list. Then, looking at the room packed with anxious people, he ran back to his car to get his wife. Within minutes they were inside and debating on whether to buy #16 or #17.

The door opened again. More customers. Chaos.

I placed sold stickers on #33 and #42 so everyone would know they were sold. Panic erupted.

The couple debating between 16 and 17 reacted to the new sold stickers and demanded I put a sticker on number 17 for them. "No one take #17—it's ours. We're buying 17," they yelled.

Closing the doors after the last group left, I sat down to try to understand what had just happened.

Typically, I sold one or two homes a month, none on a Wednesday. The real estate market wasn't hot and there were competing developments all over town.

Today, for no particular reason, people had all arrived at the same time. They entered the tiny sales trailer with little or no expectation of buying, as far as I could tell, then suddenly experienced the fear of losing out.

They reacted emotionally and purchased with no knowledge of facts, details or features. Based purely on the emotion and energy of others, each person determined a perceived value and completely disregarded the comparative process.

Emotion drove actions.

That Wednesday I sold five homes, all at full price.

I never had a chance to present a single detail about our great location, proximity to transit, special insulation, solid wood kitchen cabinets, or how well we compared to our competition. The only thing the buyers knew was the price, and that "everyone" wanted to buy. Not a single other fact was provided, yet I sold four months' worth of townhomes in a single afternoon.

Like a man raised on bread and water experiencing his first steak (or, in marketing speak, his first sizzle), there was no turning back.

I changed my approach. I tossed the comparison charts and tore up the feature sheets. Ads changed; presentations changed. Everything was now designed to generate an emotional connection between prospect and product.

I went from being a mediocre salesperson scanning the want ads to opening my own real estate marketing company, selling new home developments throughout Western Canada, as far east as Montreal, and in Hawaii, Mexico and Palm Desert. Along the way, I set sales velocity and price records and sold out dozens of projects on opening day.

When I first learned how emotion outperformed facts and features, I thought I'd discovered something completely new. I didn't realize these types of results were well documented in the field of neurometrics, the science of how our brains respond to stimuli, and, more importantly, how our reaction to emotions is based on—of all things—human evolution.

"Evolution leads the way through desire."

Deepak Chopra

CHAPTER 5

EMOTIONAL EVOLUTION AND SURVIVAL OF THE SENSITIVE

SIX MILLION-ODD YEARS AGO, when we started running in this human race, we didn't exactly sit in the food chain's pole position.

We were more like the shrimp of the Savanna, an African appetizer, a nice tasty treat with no viable defenses. We were easy picking for faster, better-equipped predators.

Yet here we are, survivors. We eluded extinction at least in part because of our ability to form groups and tribes. This meant developing our ability to emotionally relate with others. But what role did emotions play in these group connections, our survival and our evolutionary advancement?

It could be argued that our ancestors' emotional intelligence is what kept them around while other less emotionally adaptable species disappeared. Some evolutionists feel our ability to connect on an emotional level was indeed the key. Emotion kept us connected, communicating and—as groups if not individually—ahead of our competitors and predators.

Who knows? Maybe it was our emotional ability to process, relate, share and perceive the feelings of others that allowed us to connect, survive and prosper. Maybe it still is.

TOP OF THE FOOD CHAIN

ONE THING IS CERTAIN—we weren't that impressive at the beginning. So, how did we evolve from defenselessly roaming the open plains as dull-toothed, slow, ineffective hunters who existed on other predators' leftovers into our current spot atop the food chain?

One theory is that millions of years ago, we joined forces to live and hunt in groups. To do this, we needed to connect with other humans, even though our language was doubtlessly limited to a lot of grunting, nodding and pointing. (The same communication skills level I regressed to during a recent European vacation!)

Regardless of limited language skills, we early humans interacted with our tribes, reading and responding to their emotions and expressions as they acted out their stories and experiences. To survive, we had to coexist with our group by relating to their emotions. With limited language, it's reasonable to assume stories were packed with emotional expression that held the tribe's attention. It's easy to imagine how emotional communication connected us and enhanced our survival long before our linguistic skills evolved.

In his brilliant 2014 book *Sapiens, A Brief History of Humankind*, Professor Yuval Noah Harari theorizes on the origin of human beings. He describes how we outpaced other primates in the race to survive by using our ability to connect and tell stories. Other species were unable to use the emotional communication of art and storytelling, and their advancement slowed, or worse, stopped.

Now here we are, far from the savanna. We survived the harshest of elements and the most vicious predators, and along the way, developed deep emotional intelligence.

It's no wonder marketing campaigns that communicate an emotional story resonate and connect so deeply. They awaken our intuitions and primal instincts.

Unfortunately, as our communication skills developed, the better we became at presenting descriptive detail, and the further we moved from emotional connection.

Yet some persuaders understand the human brain is constantly in survival mode and that threat and reward generate the strongest emotional responses. They also know that the brain interprets one of these factors as being much more important than the other—and that's where they focus.

NOT ALL EMOTIONS ARE CREATED EQUAL

AS AN ADAPTIVE FUNCTION OF SURVIVAL, humans developed a heightened awareness, or sensitivity, for things that may have a potentially threatening outcome. We prioritize potential threat as much more important than possible reward.

Ignoring a rustling bush that **could** be hiding a saber-tooth may have a greater and more immediate consequence on our lives than not reacting to an opportunity to pick a piece of fruit.

In today's terms, this primitive imprint means we pay significantly more attention to anything potentially threatening, such as negative headlines, than we do to positive descriptions of reward.

» **The Housing Market Bubble is About to Burst**

» **These 10 Cities Will be Below Sea Level by 2030**

» **Why the Stock Market Will Collapse in 30 Days**

» **The Top Five Mistakes Every New Buyer Makes**

Even though we complain about the barrage of negative news, dire headlines still capture our attention because we are genetically predisposed to react to even the slightest potential of threat (i.e., the rustling bush).

We now filter more information at a faster rate than at any other time in our evolutionary history. Today's avalanche of information, newsfeeds, headlines, social media posts and advertising messages pours down upon us, all vying for our attention.

The result? We've become analytically impulsive.

Under constant bombardment, the regions of our brain dedicated to sorting out experiential and information input are working overtime to identify potential threats and possible rewards. But it is too large a task.

To cope with the volume, we've adopted a triage-like process and instantly prioritize incoming information to determine what receives attention and what gets dismissed.

Anything possibly damaging gets our attention. If something is presented as potentially positive, we will often put it aside for later or delete it all together. Our unconscious mind tells us that the cost of skipping an opportunity is not nearly as expensive as the cost of missing a warning.

Positive marketing may seem like it will rise above the noise. But it's good to be bad, because nasty gets noticed.

THE SEDUCTION OF NEGATIVITY

OUR REACTION TO THE NEGATIVE IS INSTINCTUAL. We've evolved to respond emotionally to potentially harmful situations as if they were actually happening.

A well-known example is the emotional "fight or flight" reaction. Anyone giving a wedding speech to friends and family can attest to this. Logic tells us we are in a safe environment and talking to the most generous audience we will ever face. Yet, regardless of the familiarity and the smiling faces, our emotions are instinctive. They overpower our logic and we experience an adrenaline flood designed specifically for self-preservation.

Emotion overpowers logic and because we prioritize threat over reward, negativity generates more attention than positivity. This explains why the headline "The Worst Foods to Put in Your Body" is clicked on significantly more often than "The Best Foods You Can Eat."

The science of neurobiology, how our nervous system affects behavior, supports the theory that our amygdala (the section of our brain responsible for detecting threat and reward) assigns values to our experiences.

In the case of positive stimuli, our amygdala assigns a value to the experience **after** it has occurred. Whereas when we encounter negative stimuli, like a potential threat, it is assigned a perceived value **before** it happens. **This is why persuaders use fear of loss—it is often experienced immediately.**

Negative stimuli =

evaluated *before* it's experienced

Positive stimuli =

evaluated *after* it's experienced

Fear is our most powerful emotion because our brains assign fear of loss **the same value as actual loss**. Thus, even the mere potential of loss becomes a vital tool in persuasion and emotional manipulation.

Simply put, evolution has designed us to be constantly focused on survival. We are therefore hyperalert to anything that potentially signals or could assist us in a harmful situation.

Negativity prompts our primal instinct to sit up and pay attention.

Some studies suggest negative stimuli influence our response mechanisms five times more powerfully than positive stimuli. It is a ratio I believe in. From personal experience, I've seen how negative marketing grips attention and overpowers common sense.

But there's more to it than engaging attention with negative stimuli. Yes, you can use nasty headlines to evoke emotion and attract your audience—but if you want to inspire their behavior, you have to do more.

It's a concept many misunderstand. Too often, campaigns place too much emphasis on "opening rates" and "views" as the only metrics of success and rely completely on presenting the negative. This may generate a collection of thumbs-ups and likes, but it won't deliver action or sales.

Negative stimuli may generate an initial reaction but there are a few more steps that need to be implemented if your aim is to influence.

The first is to include a positive emotional reward.

Negative marketing generates initial attention, but your audience is left associating your offering with negative emotions. By offsetting the negative trigger with a **positive emotional reward**, you can attract your audience AND leave them in a positive state of mind.

» The Housing Market Bubble is About to Burst
and here's how you will profit

» **These Ten Cities Will be Below Sea Level by 2030**
and the five safest places to live on earth

» **Why the Stock Market Will Collapse in 30 Days**
and how to profit

» **The Top Five Mistakes Every New Buyer Makes**
and how to avoid them

Attraction is important, as is a positive association with your offering. But to convert an audience's initial interest into action, your messages must also be deeply relevant.

RELEVANCE

IN THE SAME WAY OUR LIMITED CAPACITY to manage incoming stimuli motivates us to focus on the negative more than the positive, humans focus their available attention on whatever has the greatest personal relevance.

The deeper a message resonates with your market, the stronger its effect. Just ask a PETA member if they'd rather donate to house the homeless or ban animal testing. Both worthy causes, yet relevance will play a large role in the response.

Regardless of your offering, if your audience doesn't relate to your messaging (identified threat or potential reward) you won't entice interest or produce results. (Later, we'll discuss how to engage an uninterested audience.)

PARTICIPATION

WHEN WE'RE PROMISED A REWARD that requires our participation, the reward becomes much more valuable.

General Mills, the owner of the Betty Crocker brand, increased cake mix sales dramatically when they removed an ingredient and asked homemakers to add an egg. By doing so, they created a greater feeling of achievement, increasing the emotional value of the cake.

For a more current example, just spend a little time in IKEA's kitchen design area. Witness the hordes hovering over computer stations, clicking and dragging cabinet options across their screens in an act of self-directed interior design. Listen to the printers whirr as they spit out the new kitchen layouts, complete with a treasure map of in-store product locations needed to complete the process.

The time and expertise invested in the creation of their new IKEA kitchen is relatively small, yet from the customers' vantage point, this contribution is substantial. Being able to direct their own design attaches them emotionally to the result and increases their perceived value of the end product.

General Mills got it. IKEA gets it.

Add an egg, click and drag a cabinet, answer a survey about new product direction—it's all the same. Building in customer participation increases the emotional value of your offering.

IKEA knows that customers who design their kitchens, search the aisles for their cardboard-covered treasures, pack their vehicles with Tetris-like efficiency and survive the animated instruction booklets will ultimately experience intensified emotional ownership. It is a process that increases their perception of the product's value and emotionally connects them with the brand.

Even if we secretly believe that IKEA is Swedish for garage sale, that faux-wood KALLAX storage unit we selected, searched for, transported, constructed and suffered with is, well, priceless.

CREATING HYPER-URGENCY

MANY PRESENTATIONS BALANCE THEIR NEGATIVE with a positive reward and some even offer a level of built-in customer participation that is relevant to the audience—but the most effective persuaders create a hyper-state of urgency by adding one last ingredient.

They introduce a **devil**.

» **The Housing Market Bubble is About to Burst—**
and here's how the RICH will profit

» **These 10 Cities Will be Below Sea Level by 2030—**
and what POLITICIANS know about the five safest places to live on earth

» **Why the Stock Market Will Collapse in 30 Days—**
and how STOCKBROKERS will benefit

» **The Top Five Mistakes Every New Buyer Makes—**
and how FOREIGN INVESTORS avoid them

The best persuaders know they must first capture our attention by presenting a negative that resonates, then balance this with a positive reward. They know that the introduction of a devil emotionally connects the audience to an unknown, and when they align an action **against this devil** as a way to earn that positive reward, the result is hyper-urgency.

"...the oldest and strongest kind of fear is fear of the unknown"

H.P. Lovecraft

CHAPTER 6

ANGELS AND DEVILS

THE AMERICAN WRITER H.P. LOVECRAFT, quoted on the facing page, understood human behavior. He based much of his work on the emotion of fear for good reason: it's our most powerful motivator. When passion (desire to act) is united with fear of an unknown, the emotional combination is intensely motivating.

But Lovecraft was far from the first to recognize this connection between the unknown and persuasion.

IT'S THE EARLY 1400S and Christianity is facing a revolt.

Famine and early death are the norm. Nearly half the population is dying of bubonic plague; the other half wants someone to blame.

The masses point at God directly, or at least indirectly, and even the most devoted begin to question their faith. The church is losing its people and power at an unprecedented rate.

With steep congregational decline and conversion numbers falling, the church is in crisis. In today's terms, we'd say that customer loyalty was evaporating, and new clients were almost impossible to find.

The church's pitch, "the joy of Heaven" versus "the everlasting anguish of Hell," was losing its emotional influence. The masses still believed, but religion's motivation wasn't translating like in the good old days. Christianity needed a marketing boost.

Part of the problem, at least, was Hell. More specifically, Hell's spokesperson, the devil. He just wasn't that scary when compared to starvation and the plague.

With only a thin description in the Bible, most people then perceived the devil as an ex-angel with poor decision-making abilities and extreme delusions of grandeur—in other words, not that intimidating.

So, the devil got a makeover.

By the 16th century, John Baptist Medina's engravings of a bat-winged, horned and hooved, trident-wielding devil accompanied the fourth edition of Dante's *Inferno*. The popular book was a narrative of the journey between Heaven, Purgatory and Hell. And just like that, the devil had a new image. Christianity developed a new pitch.

"It's okay, you don't have to convert. Oh, by the way, have you seen our underworld spokesperson, the devil? No? Ah, not to worry. If you don't join up, you'll run into him eventually."

Dante and Baptist de Medina solidified the devil's persona so strongly that the image continues to influence society more than 500 years later. It was a branding makeover so powerful that modern-day marketers could still learn a thing or two from it.

In marketing and persuasion, the devil is more than the stick that backs the incentive of the carrot. The devil is the ultimate audience unifier. Persuaders know they can connect, consolidate and control even the most diverse and unruly group by introducing a common threat.

Be it real or perceived, if it's relevant, once this threat is identified, fear of the unknown is intensely motivating. For persuaders, the devil is the enemy of inaction. Its existence corrals independent thinkers into a motivated group hell-bent on a single, focused crusade—action.

If you want your campaign to be motivating and your audience to act cohesively and with emotion, get busy creating a devil.

» **This antivirus program will save you from computer hackers.**
» **Foreign investors are buying all your region's land—and your children's future.**
» **43 people are watching this auction item right now.**
» **Seven people are currently looking at this home.**
» **Check your credit score! Thieves are stealing your identity.**
» **Increase military spending—North Korea is testing missiles at its border.**
» **Want to stop illegal aliens from stealing your jobs? Elect a candidate who will build a better border wall!**

Damn devils.

Devil leveraging. It's not new. From the Crusades to modern-day political campaigns, presenting an audience with the threat of an inconceivable force pitted against it inspires action like nothing else can. It's how mass motivation is created, and it's been happening since the dawn of time.

Strong marketing campaigns take advantage of this proven tactic. Some take it even further, using the stealthy approach of showing us how to keep things from getting worse rather than how to get better.

Pfizer's campaign for their cholesterol-lowering drug Lipitor linked cholesterol levels to heart attacks and urged patients to "know their numbers."

While heart attack risks include a wide range of factors, including hypertension, stress, obesity and high LDL cholesterol, Pfizer approached cholesterol as the devil. They portrayed the battle against this devil as ongoing—and their drug as the way to keep him at bay. Their campaigns illustrated how Lipitor helped bring cholesterol numbers under the predetermined national guidelines. The result? More than $150 billion in sales.

Identifying the evils keeping our lives from getting better is one way to use a devil. Another is to position your obstacle, or your competition, as devilish. (*Bernie Sanders is a Socialist. Refugees are gang members.*)

This approach allows you to emotionally connect your offering as an act against said devil.

It is something Apple did very well in their "Apple Guy versus PC Guy" TV advertising spots.

As part of their "Get a Mac" campaign, Apple set up two humans to playfully depict the differences between angelic (supercool) Apple and its competitor, the devilish (tragically uncool) Microsoft.

These "Hi, I'm a Mac"/"Hi, I'm a PC" ads positioned actor Justin Long as a young, confident, casual Mac against the all-business, no-fun John Hodgman, who plays the out of touch PC.

One memorable exchange starts with the PC waddling onto the screen in a suit and tie, so bloated he looks on the verge of exploding. The PC explains that he is so slow and fat from "all this trial software that they pack my hard drive full of—all these programs that don't do very much unless you buy the whole thing are just plain useless. It really slows me down." Looking for empathy, the PC says to the Mac, "You know how it is!"

Mac's response is a casual, "Actually I don't. Macs just come with the stuff you want, like iTunes, iPhoto, iWeb—it's all part of iLife."

The commercial stops abruptly when the PC needs to shuffle his zeppelin-shaped body off-screen to retrieve a forgotten item.

Microsoft's PC is depicted as past its prime, suffering from an over-inflated sense of self-importance. Apple presented its Mac as a tool for people to elevate themselves above their competitor's outdated, creativity-limiting technology. It associated its product with its audience's emotional self-image: cool, relaxed, creative and intelligent.

One ad, actually called "Angel/Devil," features Mac handing PC an iPhoto book created on an Apple. An angel and devil appear over the PC's shoulder, debating whether to destroy the book, encouraging and discouraging. Evidently, even the devil has its own devils.

Microsoft responded to Apple's advertising parodies by presenting people from all walks of life proudly stating, "I am a PC," in an effort to refute Apple's characterization.

Unfortunately, the Microsoft ads didn't connect emotionally. They focused heavily on features, with one ad called "Laptop Hunter" fixated exclusively on features and (tragically) price as their differentiators. (Booo.)

Apple's approach evoked emotion, aligned their product with the audience's brand expectations and, most importantly, positioned the act of buying their product as a win against the audiences' devil. (The fear of being uncool and out of touch.)

Persuaders use this technique to sell everything. It isn't just to get people to pay three times as much for one computer over another. The devil is used to sell everything from convincing a nation to go to war, to peddling extended warranties (ironically offered right after a presentation on product quality) to vacuum cleaners (our only chance to fight back against the unthinkable horror of dust mites).

With the devil exposed, you can align your product with the action needed to eliminate the threat, and your audience has little choice but to participate or face the hellish possibility of the unknown. Or worse—live with skin-feasting dust mites.

But first, you need to define your devil.

NAMING YOUR DEVIL

IT'S NOT ALWAYS EASY FINDING A REAL DEVIL. So, persuaders often have to conjure one up. Sound difficult? It's not. Your audience has their own devils. In fact, they'll have plenty, both real and perceived. That's good news for manipulators, because if they can't find an authentic devil, they can unearth an audience's perceived threat and achieve the same effect.

The reason a perceived devil is just as powerful as an actual devil is because of—yes, you guessed it—evolution.

From the start, humans' chances of survival have been enhanced by the fact that we experience **potential threat** as equal to or greater than **actual threat**. It is an important evolutionary trait that has kept us alive. Overreacting to a slithering stick is a better survival plan than picking it up to see why one end is rattling.

Reacting to a potential threat and imminent danger with the same intensity has improved our survival chances, but it has also made us vulnerable to the dark arts of manipulation. (Not to mention worry, anxiety, stress, jealousy and depression.)

Whether it is convincing one nation not to trust another or selling more widgets, persuaders know that a clearly identified devil is a focal point that merges their audience into a unified force against the real or threatened forces of evil.

> Sometimes the devil identifies itself. Consider the December 7, 1941, attack on Pearl Harbor. America had resisted international pressure to join the Second World War. A single Japanese military decision galvanized an entire nation into a single-focused, unstoppable force, uniting against a common threat.

Master persuaders understand that attaching fear of loss to a devil and then presenting their offering as a strike against it is powerful, whether it's selling a vacuum by showing close-ups of dust mites or a mouthwash as a cure for gingivitis—or advertising the Humvee military war vehicle as a suburban commuter offering protection against foreign invasion.[1]

WHEN IT COMES TO THREAT, SIZE DOESN'T MATTER

IF AN ACTUAL DEVIL ISN'T AVAILABLE, an implied one is just as effective. As long as it's relevant to the audience, your devil can be nationwide, or germ sized. Regardless of the devil's scale or its connection to reality, persuaders follow these manipulative steps:

---

1   After the 9/11 attacks, "Humvee" advertising included images of their truck with a roof-mounted machine gun.

1. Identify concerns relevant to the audience: e.g., enemies of freedom or personal health;
2. Animate this devil by creating a recognizable characterization: Weapons of mass destruction or food poisoning;
3. Present it as an immediate threat: They are testing nuclear weapons now; or, E. coli lives on your kitchen counters;
4. Align the solution with their purpose or product: Increased national security spending or a germ-killing cleaner;
5. Present the audience's action against the devil as the solution: Elect a pro-military candidate; buy this toxic cleaner;
6. Generate real and perceived reward for the action: feel safer from foreign attack; you've kept your family healthy.

Who wouldn't spend a few cents extra for a cleaner that keeps their family safe from deadly airborne viruses or vote for a strong leader if your nation was facing a potential war?

IT IS A POWERFUL TACTIC. Once identified and imbedded in consciousness, the devil becomes an effective tool that can be easily amplified and simply communicated.

During the 1960 presidential election, John F. Kennedy used this convincing combination to generate support for his presidential bid. He positioned the Russian military as the devil and intensified voter emotions by defining the Cold War as an immediate threat.

His platform included a strong stance on staying ahead of the Soviets in the arms race and included several warnings that America could fall behind, as the Soviet Union had more nuclear missiles.

Kennedy articulated this as a "missile gap," presenting the military mismatch as a serious threat to the American people and something other candidates simply didn't understand. A vote for Kennedy was an action against this devil and the solution to the crisis. Shortly after Kennedy was elected, the missile gap claim was denounced; the Kennedy administration admitted it didn't actually exist.

If the devil is relevant to your audience, it will influence and motivate action. We are hardwired to react, regardless of the authenticity of the threat.

In fact, fear of loss can be more powerful than actual loss because it can influence emotions forever (e.g., a lifelong fear of flying) while the emotions associated with an actual loss typically fade over time.

Our unconscious mind's inability to differentiate between potential and actual loss drives us to overreact in even the safest situations.

Peering over the edge of the high diving board, we know the water will break our fall, yet our survival system makes the next step seem impossible.

Similar survival instincts are activated when an object is perceived as desirable and its availability is limited. Suddenly, loss becomes a relevant threat. For example, we decide to buy a condo, but purchase lineups become the norm and prices begin to rise rapidly. Or shoppers empty store shelves of toilet paper at the outbreak of a pandemic. Our actions are influenced by our fear of a **potential outcome** rather than reality**.**

Once desire is stimulated, the fear of losing that toilet paper or condo feels like something that we already own is in danger of being taken away.

A SUBTLE BALANCE: THREAT AND REWARD

THERE ARE FEW THINGS as emotionally motivating as fear. But using only threat of loss will leave your audience uncertain and, in some cases, have an effect opposite to the one intended.

Over time, an audience facing loss can grow resilient, accept it and move on.

During heated housing markets, for example, hopeful home buyers repeatedly losing out to higher bids often give up looking altogether. They accept their situation rather than being motivated by it.

Over time, emotional exhaustion makes an audience more challenging to reach and even harder to persuade. The introduction of an emotional reward balances fear of loss and amplifies persuasion.

Kennedy may have used the missile gap to seize the electorate's attention, but understanding the need to balance threat with reward, he also guaranteed a commitment to social issues and economic growth. He may have warned of a troubling threat, but he also offered a promising future.

The challenge for persuaders is that fear and reward aren't equal in their influence, which makes the balancing act a tricky one.

Again, we are engineered to act **before** threat and to respond **after** reward.

In evolutionary terms, we've developed to process threat by experientially predicting its potential outcome—we're hardwired to act before a threat becomes a danger.

Reward, on the other hand, isn't experienced until after it is achieved. Once reward is experienced, neurotransmitters raise our dopamine levels to produce feelings of pleasure, which in turn encourage us to repeat the experience.

Threaten to steal $20 from someone and watch them morph into defensive mode. But tell them you intend to give them $20 and their reaction will likely be skepticism. (Unless you happen to be in a candy store with your 11-year-old; here results may vary.)

For a promised reward to elicit the same level of reaction as a potential threat, the $20 must be visible; even better, placed in the hand of the recipient. This inequality of effect means that persuaders must amplify the anticipation of reward when balancing it against a perceived threat such as fear of loss.

This is why lottery ticket sales increase as the jackpot grows, yet the odds of winning remain the same (1 in about 14 million).

When balanced correctly, threat and reward trigger an emotional reaction that exceeds their individual capacity. The two are powerful influencers when combined correctly. But there's one emotional duo that is even more powerful—the combination of inclusion and exclusion.

"People enjoy things more when they know a lot of other people have been left out."

Russ Baker, two-time Pulitzer Prize-winning satirist

CHAPTER 7

THE POWER OF INCLUSION: ARE YOU IN OR ARE YOU OUT?

AS YOU SIT IN YOUR FAVORITE RESTAURANT, the chef emerges in her whites. She walks to your table and shakes your hand. After thanking you for coming in, she returns to the kitchen without acknowledging the other tables.

Congratulations, you've achieved inclusion. But its value comes at the cost of exclusion.

If the chef had stopped and warmly greeted each table, there would be no exclusivity, no exclusion—and the emotional value of inclusion would be lost.

For inclusion to be effective, it must be balanced against some form of exclusion, real or perceived. A nightclub doorman lifting the velvet rope to let you in only has value if you've passed others waiting in line.

There is endless research dissecting the power of peer pressure, social acceptance and the magnetism of the herd. And for good reason. Our instinctual need for inclusion and our fear of exclusion are evolutionary traits that constantly dictate how we buy, act and participate.

Barack Obama's election team learned the emotional power of inclusion. During their first campaign, they delivered a simple message: "Get out the vote." After analyzing the results, they expanded the language to include, "...a record turnout is expected."

Voters were more likely to act if they knew they would be part of something big.

Whether you're enticing a national audience or running a local sales campaign, including by excluding increases urgency and demand. The key is to understand that the excluded group need only be perceived by the audience as real for the full effect to be achieved.

In order to have insiders, there must be outsiders.

Inclusion has intense emotional value that can be traced back to early human origins. To be left out of a group meant your chances of survival were greatly diminished.

This instinct still motivates humans to action:

» Join our exclusive subscribers' list to receive secret tips and valuable insights unavailable to the general public.

» Only those with appointments are allowed to buy on opening day.

» If you act now, you'll be eligible for our employee pricing.

» Join our VIP Insiders Group to receive early notice of special discounts.

Airlines are famous for leveraging exclusivity. Charging astronomical prices for first-class tickets, they seat these opulent champagne-level travelers up front before parading the rest of us past to reinforce the value for both the included and excluded groups.

Depending on the aircraft, typical seat width is approximately 18 inches in coach and 21 inches in first class, or about 14 percent larger. But it's more than just wider seats that hyper-inflates the difference in pricing.

As the economy passengers shuffle past, we get a glimpse of luxury before the curtain snaps closed, punctuating our heightened sense of exclusion. Wedging bags into overhead compartments and our adult bodies into child-sized spaces, we sit in contorted discomfort discovering that, much like our luggage, our satisfaction is lost.

Inclusion creates a higher perceived value and generates a stronger relationship with customers—something most businesses wish to achieve. By presenting a perceived exclusion, this tactic uses one group as an enticement to increase the urgency in another group, but it also has a peripheral effect. It pushes the excluded group to focus more on **achieving inclusion** than the **actual value** of the inclusion.

Will Shultz's *Fundamental Interpersonal Relationships Orientation* identifies that—in addition to our physiological need for survival—we also have the need for inclusion. We need to belong and be accepted and appreciated.

This need is stronger in some people than others, but at some level all of us need affection, acceptance and close relationships. Consider this the next time you check to see how many people gave your post a thumbs-up, or how you feel the next time a group of friends are discussing an event they all attended to which you were not invited.

In Abraham Maslow's famous hierarchy of needs, he lists inclusion (belonging) as a foundational human need, more urgent than anything other than food, water, warmth, rest and safety.

Inclusion and exclusion are powerful because they are primal and integral to our species. Being part of a tribe meant working together to secure resources, hunt and be protected. Those excluded from the group had to fend for themselves against much larger and faster predators.

Inclusion meant life or death, and those hardwired instincts have evolved into fear of possible exclusion as well as attraction to opportunities for inclusion. Because of this, we instinctively associate exclusion as a threat to our survival. This need to avoid exclusion often inflates the value of inclusion.

In many of my real estate campaigns, I've used inclusion and exclusion, only to be inundated by an intense reaction from those excluded. Whether it was a campaign to help first-time buyers enter the market that generated strong buying from investors or a campaign to attract investors that resulted in attracting a large contingent of non-investors, or a "locals only" campaign that generated intense interest from out-of-town buyers—inclusion and exclusion generated powerful emotional motivation that affected behavior.

The true power of inclusion and exclusion is that they have the emotional power to intensify value well beyond actual value—something I've experienced myself.

IN THE 2007-2008 FINANCIAL CRISIS, many Canadians considered buying U.S. property as home values south of the border fell below replacement costs. Oversupply collided with low demand and financial uncertainty, prices dropped to record lows and buying in the Southern U.S. became a common dinner table topic.

Our family was no different; buying in sunny Arizona was especially tempting.

We watched for the right opportunity, but hesitated at the realities of travel and maintenance, and finally decided against it.

Until I read an ad that changed my mind, that is.

The home, like many others, was advertised at a great price, but there was a catch. For the first week it was only available to purchasers who would be owner-occupiers. Investors and out-of-town buyers (those devils!) couldn't present their offers until the following week.

My mind raced to find ways around this exclusion. No longer considering how much we would actually use the home, the distance or how to manage upkeep, all I could think about was how to convince the seller to see me as a local, a non-investor. The week passed, the dust settled, and I realized my sudden desire to buy was motivated by an aversion to exclusion.

Exclusion and inclusion, fear of loss, reward, rejection, acceptance, threat, anxiety, empathy, anger, fear, joy, sadness, love—these are just a few of the many triggers and emotions we experience. Some are more powerful than others in guiding how we experience the world and make decisions within it, but every emotional instinct we have is attached to our evolutionary need for survival.

This is something persuaders understand. Facts and features are no match for the power of evolution.

More importantly, in their quest to influence human behavior, persuaders know that the intensity of our reaction is related to the emotional value we assign to each experience. And because every emotion is attached to our evolutionary quest for survival, trying to influence without using emotion can end in catastrophe.

CHAPTER 8

THE HIGH COSTS OF *NOT* HARNESSING EMOTION

AFTER WINNING THREE CONSECUTIVE TERMS by majority vote and bringing the 2010 Winter Olympics to Vancouver, B.C. premier Gordon Campbell was forced to resign. His downfall wasn't illegal endeavors, underhanded bribes or unscrupulous actions.

His mistake? Underestimating the power of emotion.

At the core of this catastrophe was the province's new Harmonized Sales Tax (HST). But the tax wasn't the issue—his fall from grace was triggered by the way he'd introduced the tax.

If only he'd paid attention to what happened just a few provinces over, where the HST received a much different reception. In Ontario, politicians declared that overseas competitors were causing local job losses. They simplified the challenges by describing a devil, made it relevant and emotional, then positioned the HST as a solution. The citizens of that province accepted the tax as an act of self-defense and went on to reelect the politicians responsible.

In B.C., Premier Campbell dismissed the power of emotion and introduced the HST using facts and data. No emotion, no devil—all detail. Presenting the HST as a "*proficient tax* with *negligible impact*," he delivered a solution to a problem his audience didn't know they had.

With no problem to solve, the people of the province reached their own conclusion: the new tax was a money grab.

Premier Campbell neglected to identify an emotional issue. He failed to find a devil. The more he pushed the facts of this new tax, the more the public pushed back.

Two different provinces, two different presentations of the same tax. One used emotional persuasion and was successful; the other, using only details and features, ended in catastrophe.

The B.C. HST rollout was a complicated series of announcements about how the tax was to be applied, an approach that left consumers confused and angry. Some goods and services were exempt, some were not, while others qualified for a complex sliding scale of rebates.

Dairy milk was tax-exempt, but buy rice milk and you paid HST. Lactose: Good. Rice milk: Bad. Buy six doughnuts—pay no tax. Buy a single doughnut—pay full tax.

Confusion flourished and the public grew angry. The irater people became, the more politicians responded with details like, "This new HST will save consumers a full two percent." At the same time, in what was probably an unrelated move by another government department, the tax on beer was increased by—yep, two percent. Taxing a Canadian's doughnuts and beer and not seeing how this would end was a miscalculation of epic proportion.

For businesses, it was an economic gut punch.

Restaurant owners now had to charge HST on meals. It was a small cost, but it caused a dramatic reduction in guests. Real estate developers were forced to charge HST on new homes and watched as buyers boycotted their construction projects and paid more for older homes right across the street.

Politicians, frustrated by the backlash, defended the HST as uncomplicated; the subtext was that their constituents were at fault for not understanding. It ignited a revolt, and because the public hadn't been given a devil, they chose their own—the politicians.

In the middle of this mess, I was about to market a 152-unit new home development. I needed a new approach. I needed my own devil. Fast.

GOT DEVIL?

PROPERTY DEVELOPERS INADVERTENTLY CAUGHT UP in the HST crossfire tried everything, even including the HST in their prices. But it wasn't about the tax anymore. It had become a revolt against the way government forced the new levy upon the people.

Despite our usual apologetically polite "please, thank you and I'm sorry," these Canadians had finally had enough. We were pissed. (Sorry about the profanity.) In a typical Canuck-style rebellion, we simply avoided purchasing things impacted by the new tax.

The economy staggered. The people screamed. Campbell resigned.

Premier Campbell's replacement promised a future referendum on the HST, but it didn't matter in real estate—the new home market continued to slide as the few remaining buyers decided to wait for the vote.

The referendum was scheduled to take place six months later, but my project was about to launch in few weeks. The question was how to use an emotional devil as motivation to encourage buying now. The answer came from an unlikely source—a little ski shop.

I've always been a fan of this small retailer. At the start of each ski season they had people lined up to buy, despite their competition from lower-priced, big budget, national retailers. A visit to the tiny store was an experience. Packed to the rafters with gear and overflowing with happy customers, their "Say no to Big Box!" message made you feel like buying from them was an act of happy rebellion.

Their campaign clincher: everything sold preseason was FREE if it snowed on Christmas Day.

The little shop had identified an emotional devil (the evil big box stores!) and used the possibility of future reward to drive immediate sales. The combination meant business was booming and they could sell at higher prices than the competition; keeping profit margins higher meant it was possible to attract and retain the kind of helpful, informed staff that kept customers loyal.

Studying their approach gave me all I needed:

» They identified an emotional devil that was relevant to their audience (the heartless international retailers);

» They presented buying as an act of rebellion against this devil;

» They offered a potential future reward to build excitement, create immediate demand, and more importantly, earn free media coverage;

» They used the potential of future possibilities as a reason to buy today;

» They generated urgency by offering this opportunity only during the preseason;

» They used emotion to overpower the need to compare prices.

BETTING ON EMOTION

IT WAS AN EASY STRATEGY TO CONVERT. The government had unwittingly become a devil toward which the province's residents felt intense emotion. I positioned the act of purchasing in our development as an act of rebellion against this devil. The opportunity to act was limited in time, occurring only on our grand opening sales day.

Our controversial stance against the tax became a public relations and media magnet.

A few weeks later, staring back at a bank of TV cameras and a room full of reporters, I was at a podium.

"We don't believe in the HST, and we refuse to charge it, collect it or remit it."

The reaction was as predicted—insane. It was exactly what the buyers wanted to hear. The media, tired of the same story line, latched onto the rebellious "NO HST," and it became a media rocket ship that captivated the audience.

On opening day, buyers swarmed the sales center. All 152 condominiums sold out in 152 minutes. We wrote over 200 back-up contracts (the real estate developer's equivalent of a committed waiting list) and our price per foot soared above the competitors'.

Emotion, it would seem, is a devilishly powerful motivator.

If the tax hadn't been voted out, the HST would have been pulled from the developer's profits, but the people of B.C. did vote it out. The markets recovered, the revolt subsided, and once again we could buy a single doughnut without suffering the oppression of a provincial sales tax.

We effectively used an emotional devil on a small scale, but this strategy can be used on a national audience as well.

In the 2016 U.S. elections, one political machine understood the power of mass emotional manipulation better than the other.

Donald Trump connected with voters by identifying and matching their perceptions, priorities and existing beliefs.

It's challenging to find examples of detail in Trump's campaign, but there's emotion. Lots of it. Controversies such as The Wall and views on "illegal aliens" were planted like seeds in a garden designed to grow enough shared rage and devils to feed a nation.

We knew about the wall, its emotional content flowing beyond borders north and south. But how much, how long, how high, how to secure it, construct it, maintain it—even how it would work, given the country has oceans on two sides—the facts were conveniently unavailable.

Whether you are for it or against it, Trump's presentation is purely emotional. By avoiding details and focusing the audience on the emotions connected to "keep them out!" he has amassed power and attention.

It's an essential lesson for everyone who wants to motivate or inspire. Regardless of the size of your audience, the cost of presenting facts and features without relating emotionally is disastrous.

Get it right—use emotion to persuade—and the results can be, well, "Huuge."

CHAPTER 9

INTENSIFYING EMOTIONAL VALUE AND DEMAND

"Who'll pay me $6 for this? Okay, fine, how about $5?"

No one responded.

"It's a real $5 bill," I assured them, holding up the money. "What if I lowered my price to $4?" No one budged.

It's the reaction I'd hoped for.

I'd been asked by the owner of several real estate companies to speak with his agents about increasing the audience's perception of their value.

My first step was to dissect the connection between value and price.

The fact is that no one will pay $6 for a $5 bill, because we all believe deeply that the value of a $5 bill is five bucks. As a matter of fact, no one sees logic in paying $5 for a $5 bill. Why bother? Where it gets interesting is that no one would even pay $4 for a $5 bill.

Our confidence in the bill's value is so strong that lowering my price to $4 only evoked feelings of mistrust because it challenged the audience's perception.

We believe value is based on comparative facts and features. So, most of us think that to change a perception, such as your audience's value of your product or service, we must give them more, bigger, better facts and features.

I've won these awards. I listed and sold X-number of homes. I am a hard worker and tireless marketer. I care about representing you. I advertise every week and have a team of talented people to serve you. I represent only the finest homes. Fact. Fact. Fact. Feature. Feature. Feature. Bigger, better, more.

And on we go, presenting details in an effort to change an audience's perception of our value. But it doesn't work. Perception isn't related to facts, features or details. It's related to how we feel about each of those things. It's related to emotion.

It is human nature to hold onto our preconceived beliefs when encountering new facts. For instance, when choosing a realtor, a homeowner may consider facts for comparison purposes. But these facts on their own won't increase the homeowner's perception of the agent's value.

Without emotional influence, we judge value against our existing perception. Five bucks is only worth five bucks, nothing more, nothing less.

So, the question is, how do we increase the audience's emotional perception of our value. The answer? Attach our brand to something of higher emotional relevance to the audience.

I pointed to a woman in the back. "You seem like a trustworthy, hardworking agent. I'm going to give you this $5. But first, I'm going to do something for you." I paused and wrote on the bill.

Handing her the money, I said, "To double your income this year, the only two things you need are increased emotional value and what I have written on this bill."

I handed it over and said, "All I need to know is if you agree."

She read the bill and said, "Yes."

"Keep the bill in a place you can look at it each day but never show it to anyone," I added.

She agreed.

"Okay," I continued. "Before I move on, is anyone a bit curious as to what was on that $5 bill?"

There was a resounding chorus of response. "Yes!"

Pulling out another $5 bill, I said, "Fine, I'll do it one more time. I'll write down the same information but I'm auctioning this one off for charity. Again, the winner can't share this secret with anyone. I'll give the bill to the first person who wants it for $20."

Everyone's hands went up.

Holding up the bill, I said, "Your income level is connected to your audience's emotional perception of your value. If your service is relevant to the audience, then with an increased emotional value, the only other thing needed is written on the bill. It's '**Just you**.'"

Earlier, no one would pay $5, even $4, for my $5 bill. Moments later, the perceived value of the bill escalated, and everyone wanted it because it had emotional relevance. Its perceived value quadrupled.

If emotion can increase the perceived value of something as well established as a $5 bill, it can certainly influence an audience's perception of your value.

THE MOTIVATIONAL VALUE OF EMOTION

WE'VE ALL PAID WAY TOO MUCH FOR SOMETHING we absolutely had to own, like the Bowflex Trainer that now functions as a sweater hanger in my bedroom. Its features convinced me that the product was functionally useful, but it was emotion that made me believe buying it would make me use it and using it would transform the un-transformable. I didn't buy an exercise machine, I bought confidence at the beach.

Value isn't related to price. It's related to emotion.

While it may be hard to accept that the price of anything is equal only to its perceived emotional value, it's a principle we understand instinctually.

Think of the author selling her book for $19 and her full-day course for $199. You buy the book and are impressed. While waiting for her next book, you discover she has created a course and you decide to take it.

The next book is projected to take her a year to write. The course, on the other hand, took the author only a few weeks to create.

Chances are, no matter how much you liked her first book, you wouldn't pay $199 for her second one. And even though you would own it forever, could read it over and over, refer to it anytime, highlight the important parts, or even lend it out—$199 for a book is nuts.

Is the value of the course really 10 times greater than the book? Certainly not in terms of the value of creative input.

The difference is the value of emotion. The perceptions associated with the course have an emotional connection far greater than the book, regardless of the time the book took to create or the cost of design and printing. The course means interacting with the author and—in theory— gaining a deeper understanding of her message and concept. The course's value is based on emotional perception, and that dictates its monetary value.

Having a higher perceived value will impact your monetary value, so it only makes sense (and dollars and cents) to elevate the audience's perception of your value. For that, you only need two ingredients: relevance and emotional connection.

If it's relevant, your audience will pay attention, and if it's emotional, they will pay more for it.

Let's consider the question of how relevance and emotional perception impact value by looking at another product, anchovies.

Do you like anchovies? If so, you're among a select few. Those fishy little devils, depending on opinion, can make or break a Caesar salad or pizza.

For argument's sake, let's say you detest them, and I happen to be selling these stinky mini-minnows for $20 a tin in my anchovy store.

If you're truly not a fan, there's little chance you'd be a buyer.

But wait! What if, **for a limited time**, I reduced them to $5 a tin and my call to action was, "Act fast—I have a limited supply!"

Would you buy a tin? No? What if I priced them at $1 each? How low would the cost have to be before you'd buy?

If the tins were just pennies apiece, and you remembered your sister-in-law liked the odd anchovy, there would be relevance, but still no emotion. At this price, perhaps you'd buy a few tins.

Because you're not an anchovy fan, the price doesn't matter. So, price reductions have little effect on your motivation to purchase (and the "act now" call-to-action has even less effect). But what if the presentation became personally relevant—and emotional?

Let's say you see a TV news program about a recent scientific discovery on how our lifespan is extended by anchovy consumption.

The news story showed peer-reviewed medical studies and images of people lined up outside stores across the country, pushing and shoving to buy anchovies. You even scrolled past a story about insurance companies lowering their rates for anchovy consumers because they helped people live about one extra month per tin consumed.

Hypothetically, would you consider buying a tin or two? Even if you didn't like anchovies?

If you knew me and saw the huge lineup waiting for my store to open, would you ask if you could get in ahead of the line?

Inside my store, would you negotiate on the price per tin or just pay what I was asking? Even if I'd increased the price to $40 per tin? (I am, after all, an anchovy capitalist.) Would you consider buying as many as you could, perhaps to give to your friends and family? Or, perhaps you'd buy dozens of tins and resell them to the panicking people in the line—who were acting like they would pay thousands per tin? Would you be upset to discover there was a limit of one tin per customer?

Yes, a ludicrous example. Who would ever buy a food and feed it to their kids, regardless of its horrid taste, because scientific data and media reports presented it as healthy?

Well, as kids, many of us were force-fed fried liver once a week. Research stated that eating a cow's large poison-filtering organ was good for us.

If it's emotionally relevant, demand is amplified and the audience's focus on affordability becomes concern about availability.

CHAPTER 10

CREATING EMOTIONAL CONTAGION

3, 2, 1 ... THE SPACE SHUTTLE CHALLENGER is launched on its maiden flight, Microsoft launches what would become the world's most popular word processing program, and Motorola changes the future of communication by launching the first mobile phone.

It's 1983, and the summit of the Cold War. People around the globe watch with heightened anxiety as the East and West threaten to launch world-ending missiles. Soviet early-warning systems falsely report that the U.S. has launched missiles at Russia.

Tense times.

But missile threats didn't spark the year's most violent riots, fistfights and pandemonium. What did?

Cabbage Patch Kids.

In the middle of 1982, toy company Coleco introduced their new Cabbage Patch dolls in a media-fueled campaign that set industry records.

The dolls were in such demand that people camped overnight in parking lots and stormed display aisles as the doors opened.

A woman's leg was broken, crushed by a crowd of 1,000 people crawling over each other in a mad toy-shopping scramble. Riots broke out often, and levelheaded adults lost all sense while trying to grab a doll.

People tailed trucks and hid in loading bays waiting for the arrival of the Cabbage Patch Kids deliveries, then rushed inside the store to fight for their purchase. Christmas shoppers bought an average of three dolls each, stores were massively understocked, and within months of their first appearance, the two million dolls manufactured had sold out. Scalpers resold the dolls for six times their original price. In less than two years, more than 18 million Cabbage Patch Kids were sold. The desire to own a Cabbage Patch Kid was an emotional contagion.

The phenomenon was the result of a media strategy that connected an emotion to a product, and most importantly, connected this emotion to parents and kids.

What the persuaders behind the strategy understood better than most was that the best way to increase desire is to present an object's impact on the emotions of others. Emotion is infectious.

Humans are a talented bunch. Subconsciously interpreting nonverbal communication is a visceral reaction that happens before we even have a chance to think. We've evolved to identify other people's anxiety, a survival skill that alerts us to imminent danger or potential reward.

If we are in a crowd of people with an elevated sense of anticipation, our unconscious sees the crowd's emotion as being more important than our own. Thinking goes offline while we temporary adopt the crowd's momentum and personality. We can't help it. It's evolution.

As the last hunter in a group of cavemen, say you hold the rear position while those ahead disappear into the dense jungle. With your spear held high, you stand ready to throw it at anything that looks like food.

Suddenly, the other hunters emerge from the trees and run past you, screaming in terror. If you are reading this right now, congratulations—your ancestors were among those who adopted the crowd's mentality rather than those holding onto their independent thought.

The Cabbage Patch Kid emotional contagiousness was the creation of Richard Weiner Inc., a New York PR firm that received a Silver Anvil, the industry's most prestigious award, for its role in igniting this consumer hysteria.

The PR firm sent dolls to every major media outlet and women's magazine in the country, landing segments on TV network shows, including the CBS Morning News, Nightline and the Phil Donahue Show. There was an editorial in the *Wall Street Journal*. Ultimately, Cabbage Patch Kids ended up on the *Today Show*, where pregnant host Jane Pauley appeared live with a doll for a full five minutes.

Next, the dolls were introduced to the general media in a publicity circuit that included press conferences at the Central Park Zoo and the Boston Children's Museum. In front of a bank of reporters and TV cameras, 200 ecstatic schoolchildren took part in a mass adoption ceremony to receive their dolls.

The cameras and journalists captured the emotional elation of each child as they finally received their adopted doll. Just think about how their excitement affected parents across the country watching the news coverage.

The story wasn't about a product, but about the effect the dolls had on the children receiving them. The media presented the mass emotion in a way that no advertising campaign could, and the public demand skyrocketed.

The national media dubbed it "Dollmania." *Newsweek* featured a young girl squeezing her Cabbage Patch doll on their front cover, dedicating their top story to the "Cabbage Patch Panic Phenomenon."

The dolls were mass-produced, yet no two were alike. Each had its own unique combination of skin tone, hair, eye color and clothing style. Every box contained a "one-of-a-kind doll," complete with its unique name and adoption papers. Inside the see-through packaging, the dolls reached out with open arms.

When the manufacturer's communication director, Barbara Wruck, was asked for her take on the doll craze, her response was, "They elicit strong feelings of emotion."

Demand outpaced supply. Eventually black-market sales grew to 10 times the original retail price. The media fueled the flames with continued reports of adults fighting over the dolls and the underground doll market. The consumer's desire for doll ownership and their fear of loss intensified. (And you thought anchovy hysteria was a silly concept!)

The marketing attached these rather homely little dolls to an emotion so contagious it swept the nation. The media sought analytical insight from psychiatrist David Reskoff, who presented his theory that mothers and fathers tied their self-worth as parents to their ability to acquire a doll for their children.

Marketing is about the creation of a deep emotional connection between consumer and product; media reports of frenzies at retail outlets presented images of obsessive consumerism. Viewers became subconsciously infected with the contagion. Their feelings were manipulated.

"All these people can't be wrong," was the basis of the contagion.

What started as just a toy became an instrument of self-recognition, reward and a validation of parental affection. In other words, it had little to do with the toy's features or functions and everything to do with emotions.

What I learned from Dollmania was that emotional connection is effective—and if you want to create emotional contagiousness, begin by showing your audience other people having an emotional experience.

PRESENTING THE EMOTIONAL REACTIONS of others interacting with a product was a strategy I wanted to employ in my own business.

I was lucky enough to see it work firsthand. But seeing a woman sitting on the floor pretending to have a bath amid a crowd of potential buyers was something even I didn't plan on.

But before I tell you about that, I have to tell you about buffalo.

Lots and lots of buffalo.

Herds of the hairy beasts. Young and old; in groups and alone. Some standing, some lying, others grazing. Not a care in the world. All photographed by my father on trips through the Canadian Prairies.

Then, suddenly, upside down.

"Sorry, here. Let me fix that. Damn picture is in wrong again," Dad would say as he searched for the rogue slide hidden in our projector's rotating tray.

Long before selfie sticks, Instagram Stories or Facebook Video, images were captured, developed in a darkroom, sorted and then shared via slide projector. It was a regular Saturday night event, at least at our house.

My brother and I, stylish in our onesies, a bowl of popcorn between us, sat giggling uncontrollably while we waited for the slide we had secretly flipped upside down.

Small victories.

Inevitably Dad's sorting, searching and cursing would nudge the projector's leg beyond the coffee table's edge, repositioning the buffalo into three-dimensional shapes bending at the floor and forming to the contours of our furniture.

My three-dimensional buffalo experience had been long forgotten until a meeting with a graphics company brought it back in full.

Reviewing the digital renderings for a high-rise tower I was about to sell, I asked a naive question. "If we can project these interior renderings onto a screen, couldn't we project them onto the floor and wall to create a 3D effect?"

The answer was no.

I hate hearing no.

I explained my 3D buffalo memory. The answer was still no. The angles couldn't be calibrated to match the wall and floor intersection.

"Can we at least project an image of each home's plan onto the floor in full scale?"

Yes!!

The result was "In-Real Theater," a low-tech solution for presenting new home floor plans. Computers and projectors were installed in the ceiling to illuminate each home's plan on the floor. Visitors selected their home, and with the tap of a finger on a touch screen, the plan appeared in full-scale like a giant blueprint on the floor.

At the same time, projectors presented a 24-hour time-lapsed video of the surrounding views onto the theater walls. This correlated with each floor plan so visitors could watch the sunset in their living room and see the sunrise moments later while standing in their bedroom.

Each new visitor had an opportunity to walk their floor plan and see their exact view. The press loved the concept, and their coverage showed people's ecstatic interaction with this new way of experiencing presale home buying.

Like Dollmania, the critical component was the media coverage of people's emotional reaction, from the major evening news channels to the large newspapers and smaller affiliates.

In-Real Theater, and more importantly, the public's reaction to it, became a hot industry topic. People arrived with expectations of excitement in the weeks leading up to our first sales day.

Visitors walked room to room through the projected floor plans and unrolled their cutouts of traced furniture to see how it would fit in each room. And yes, one woman sat down on the floor in the bathtub's projected outline and pretended to have a bath—or at least see how far she had to reach for her shampoo.

On opening day, potential buyers circled the block. Within hours, every suite in the tower had sold at record prices.

Perhaps an outline of a floor plan (or a bathtub) didn't motivate buyers— but seeing the emotional reaction of others certainly did.

CHAPTER 11

EMOTIONAL ANCHORS

THE LIGHTS DIMMED. The crowded theater faded to silence.

It was 1989, the movie was *Dead Poets Society*, and like everyone else, I was excited to see it because it starred Robin Williams.

The trailers presented Williams in a dramatic role as an English teacher at an all-boys school. His unorthodox teaching style contrasted with the school's deep-seated tradition as he pushed students to pursue their dreams.

The film began with a background of whispered voices and images of parents preparing their children for the first day at this elite establishment of higher learning. There was no humor, just the gravity of quiet expectation placed upon these young boys.

The cameras panned across the school's wood-paneled auditorium and down a long row of stern-looking teachers, finally stopping on Robin Williams' expressionless face.

The theater erupted in laughter. I laughed as well. How could you not? After all, it was Robin Williams.

The movie's message, "Carpe diem!" left a powerful impression on everyone, but what captured my thinking was the audience's response to Williams' image. He was funny. We saw him. We laughed. Unconscious reactions caused by an existing belief, and all of it connected to an emotional anchor.

It's a situation we face every day. Emotional anchors, set by our preexisting perception biases, subconsciously determine our reactions.

These anchors are almost impossible to unhook with rationale. Even reality fails to break the chains. Information that aligns with our beliefs is received while that which doesn't is filtered.

Still, many people continue to believe the best way to dislodge an audience from a deeply anchored belief is to counter it with strong details and facts. The result is often frustration when existing beliefs remain as strong as before—often becoming even more deeply entrenched.

While facts can be overturned with contradicting evidence, emotions are anchored deeply and keep us connected to our beliefs even when they are irrational.

The science behind why our beliefs are so intransigent is based on our preestablished "confirmation bias." Neural scientists explain that we hold on to our opinions because of our uncomfortable existence with cognitive dissonance (discomfort caused by having simultaneously conflicting beliefs). Changing a deeply held opinion calls other beliefs into question, something we humans find incredibly unsettling.

The instinct to embrace information that supports our beliefs and reject anything that contradicts it is something we come by naturally.

Jonas Kaplan, a psychologist at the University of Southern California, recently likened our reaction when receiving information that conflicts with our beliefs to that of defending against an attack. Kaplan explains,

"The brain's primary responsibility is to take care of the body, and to protect the body. (Because) the psychological self is the brain's extension of that, when our 'self' feels attacked, our [brain is] going to bring to bear the same defenses that it has for protecting the body."

In short, when our opinions are threatened, we hunker down in our position—often with little understanding of the reasoning behind our belief. So if you have an emotional bond with an existing brand, when a competing brand attempts to convert you with factual evidence of their product superiority, their efforts will have no influence. Their only chance to unhook your emotional anchor is to leverage emotion.

In a recent experiment at Yale, graduate students were asked to rate their understanding of the functionality of common items such as zippers and toilets. Ratings were high. Then in a cheeky twist, the students were asked to follow up their rating with a detailed written description of each object's operation. Who knew, toilets are really complicated.

Where zippers and toilets are concerned, believing you have a competent understanding of their operation system isn't all that dangerous. But what about religious or political beliefs, social issues, parenting or health care? Ever dug your heels in and presented points you weren't really confident in just because you were under attack by someone with a countering opinion? Most of us have. *Have not! Have too!*

The main challenge in changing an audience's opinion is that the information presented is received through preset emotional filters and existing beliefs.

CHANGE HOW PEOPLE FEEL, NOT HOW THEY THINK

AT THE BASE OF MOST DISAGREEMENTS are opposing opinions. Changing another's opinion requires that you first understand that each person's emotional anchor is deeply connected to their experience, emotions and preexisting beliefs. The core components in changing someone's opinion, be it to sell a product or to enforce a set bedtime or a list of chores, are the same as the core tactical components of persuasion. Here, facts have no influence, but emotion does.

At the risk of using too many movie analogies, the classic 1957 film *12 Angry Men* is a magnificent example of using emotion to change how people feel rather than how they think.

The movie follows a 12-person jury as they debate the fate of a young man accused of murder. Henry Fonda plays the single juror refusing to concur with the otherwise unanimous guilty verdict. The film follows his path as he gradually influences the remaining 11 jurors to vote not guilty.

Fonda persuades them, one by one, not with contradicting facts but by uncovering their emotions related to the facts, then challenging their perception. By introducing the possibility that their feelings, while reasonable, could be wrong, he emotionally makes space for other possibilities.

Every day, from getting the kids to eat their veggies to selling our widgets, we face audiences that need to be persuaded. The key in changing opinions rests in understanding the audience's position, empathizing with it, validating it and offering the potential that there may be an alternative worth considering. If you first acknowledge their opinions have validity, you connect on an emotional level and make it easier for each person to acknowledge that their position may not be the only one.

Good persuaders begin by understanding their audience's position, then provide them with an alternative.

In *12 Angry Men*, when a juror says, "You can go on talking for a hundred years and I still won't change my mind. He's guilty," Fonda's response is to agree the accused may be guilty. He then suggests there also may be another way of looking at the facts in front of them.

By acknowledging that the other juror could be right, Fonda's character provides an opportunity to consider another position without conflict. He uses a technique practiced by the ancient warrior Sun Tzu and the popular modern-day psychologist Jordan Peterson. Before they lay siege, they empathize with their target and provide them with an escape route.

If your goal is to have your opponent abandon their current position, then attacking with contradicting facts isn't effective. Escape routes must be provided, and existing beliefs must be validated. Most importantly, a new, more powerful emotion must be introduced.

Effective persuaders adjust their presentations to make them emotionally appealing to their audience. To make an alternative more appealing, it must be a better option emotionally. Getting someone to agree they are wrong is virtually impossible; getting them to agree that their viewpoint is conceivable and therefore another viewpoint is also conceivable prepares an opening in which to introduce a new, more relevant emotion.

Fonda's character doesn't contradict the other jurors by insisting the accused was innocent. His approach starts with a simple, vulnerable expression of feeling. He says that he doesn't feel it's right to condemn someone of murder without more discussion.

This is contested by the other jurors but not rejected. If Fonda had approached the other jurors by first disagreeing with them and then presenting an alternative view of not guilty, the 11 jurors would have strengthened their resolve, banded together, dug in and remained unmoved.

Jordan Peterson uses this approach well. He refers to it as "empathetic understanding" and he achieves it by reaching an understanding of the other person's point of view. Often summarizing their opinion and openly admitting they may have a valid point, he acknowledges that he understands how their perspective has been formed. This presents him as a considerate, active listener. Most importantly, it opens an opportunity for his opposition to accept a contradicting opinion. Jordan Peterson's approach is effective at converting opinions, or at the very least, improving the opportunity to present his own.

This isn't new thinking. Sun Tzu understood it more than 2,500 years ago.

The story goes that, upon surveying a castle, Sun Tzu recognized that his army dramatically outnumbered the small opposition inside. Victory was inevitable, but a lengthy siege would band the opposition together and increase their resistance. Ultimately, he would have to raze the fortress to the ground during the attack, leaving his army vulnerable while he rebuilt. His objectives were to take and hold the enemy's position, and he couldn't accomplish both by delivering a direct attack.

Sun Tzu ordered his generals to display the full breadth of the army's strength and size by setting up their camps only in front of the castle and preparing for an all-out siege. The generals quietly questioned leaving the rear of the fortress completely unguarded but acted as ordered. They were amazed to find the castle vacant and intact in the morning.

Sun Tzu's approach was to empathize with his enemy's position, show a strong front and present them with an escape route.

He knew that if the generals had surrounded the castle and presented the facts—our numbers are superior, you have limited provisions and we have you surrounded; surrender or die—it was likely the enemy's emotional fortitude would have been triggered, readying them for a long fight. The outcome would have been costly for both sides.

Like the soldiers in the fortress, our opinion certainly is fiercely defended, because it's critical to our survival. Our preset beliefs enable us to project expected outcomes during complex circumstances without time-consuming cognitive processing. It's how we can navigate a left turn through a multilane intersection without having to consider all of the complex probabilities.

This need for certainty, constructed on limited information, is often referred to by behavioral scientists as heuristic processing. Heuristic decisions, based in part on our past experiences, form the mental short-cuts needed to navigate typical everyday situations.

Capturing a castle, changing an opinion and shifting a juror's decision from guilty to not guilty is less difficult if your opponent's position has been validated first. It gets even easier if they've been given a conflict-free opportunity to retreat from their position through an introduction to a relevant and much more powerful emotion.

Consider the difference between a confrontational, factual attack and an emotional approach offering an escape route.

"You're an idiot to pay so much at Starbucks for a basic cup of coffee when Tim Hortons is right across the street, with great coffee for much less money."

"Starbucks has great coffee; I can understand why you drink it. Tim Hortons has great coffee as well, and I like knowing that every year I save enough to buy a new pair of runners."

In the brand wars, this approach is too often dismissed.

Pepsi could do all the blind taste tests in the world and still not unhook the emotionally anchored Coke drinkers (until Coca-Cola self-sabotaged by introducing New Coke and destroying the emotional bond it had worked so hard to create).

By offering emotional validation, you are not weakening your position, only acknowledging and recognizing that your audience's opposing belief, for them, is a true perspective.

On a psychological level, validation responds to the human need for self-actualization, self-esteem and acceptance (love and belonging).

All of which sit atop ol' Maslow's pyramid-shaped hierarchy of needs and follow his basis of human motivation.

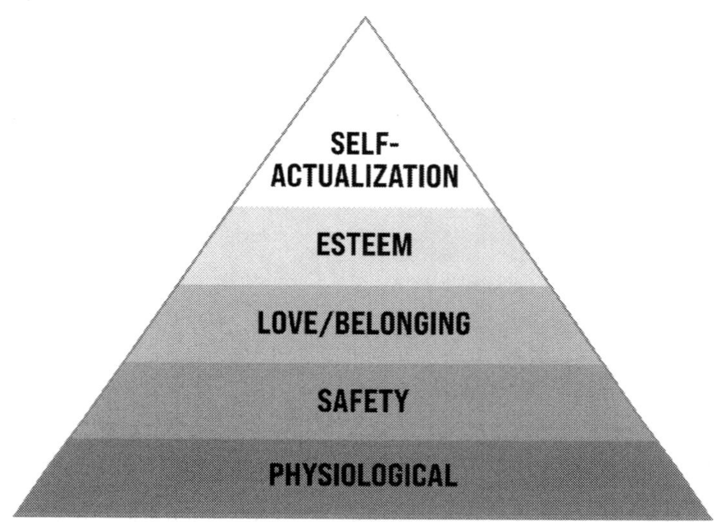

Consider political debates between Democrats and Republicans, or liberals and socialists, or capitalists and communists, each trying to alter the other side's opinion by presenting opposing facts. These efforts only strengthen their opponents' conviction and beliefs.

For that matter, consider debating bedtime with your nine-year-old. (A lot of politicians could learn a thing or two by debating my kids).

To change an anchored emotional perception, it is critical we avoid responding with rationale. "Because I said so, that's why, now go to bed" is a pretty good example of poor emotional persuasion. (Sigh.)

Instead, empathize with the emotion, validate the other's opinion and present the possibility that an alternative might exist. Once that common ground is found, introduce a relevant emotion strong enough to replace the emotion supporting the initial perception.

EMPATHY + EMOTION

A WEEK BEFORE THE 1980 PRESIDENTIAL ELECTION, 80 million viewers watched Ronald Reagan and Jimmy Carter square off during their televised debate. It was the final event in an intense race between the two candidates.

With most polls showing the outcome too close to call, the two politicians stepped on stage for one final chance to win undecided voters.

Both candidates used familiar tactics. Carter focused on critiquing the details of Reagan's policies. Reagan focused on empathy and emotion.

Reagan managed to turn a six-point gap into a historic 10-point victory by employing the art of emotional persuasion. He began by empathizing with the audience's impending challenge, having to decide who would make a better president. Then he reframed the decision from a rational one into an emotional one with a series of questions.

"Next Tuesday, all of you will go to the polls and make a decision. I think when you make that decision, it might be well if you would ask yourself, are you better off than you were four years ago? Is there more or less unemployment in the country than there was four years ago? Do you feel that our security is as safe, that we're as strong as we were four years ago?

And if you answer all of those questions yes, why then, I think your choice is very obvious as to whom you will vote for.

If you don't agree, if you don't think that this course that we've been on for the last four years is what you would like to see us follow for the next four, then I could suggest another choice that you have."

By identifying and empathizing with the audience's challenge—who to vote for—then introducing a relevant emotion by asking whether they **felt** better off than they had four years before, he connected emotionally and avoided factual comparisons. As Sun Tzu would say, he won the battle without going to war.

Reagan didn't attack Carter with facts about the slow economy, or fire off stats about high unemployment, or launch details related to declining national security. He asked, simply, emotionally, if the people felt better or worse about these things.

Then he introduced a powerful, relevant emotion. Hope.

"Do you want it to be better moving forward?"

Reagan used a three-phase approach:

1. Identify and empathize with the audience's issues,
2. Reframe the issue from fact-based to emotion-based, and
3. Introduce a more powerful, relevant emotion.

According to Gallup polls, just 10 months before Reagan became the 40th U.S. president, he was losing in the polls by an impossible 33 percent to Carter's 62 percent. Often called the "Great Communicator," perhaps the persuasive Ronald Reagan should also be remembered as the "Emotional Communicator."

GREAT EMOTIONAL COMMUNICATION

REAGAN FACED AN OVERWHELMING CHALLENGE, but he understood the true power of emotional communication and used it to change public opinion on a national scale. It was a great lesson and something I would learn to rely upon in my own little corner of the world.

I didn't need to change the minds of a nation, but I did need to change the way local residents felt about a new condominium tower project. For that, I thought, maybe I could use some of what I learned from studying

Reagan to change the public's opinion about buying in a rough neighborhood with an even tougher reputation—in a slow market.

The huge development's first three towers consisted of over 1,000 condos, but the area was one people tried to avoid, not move into. The crime problems and police incidents were in the news daily. Regardless of recent area improvements, presenting positive facts would only contradict current public perception, create mistrust and solidify resolve.

The public's negative perception of the area was deeply entrenched and not going to change before the towers were built. To unhook this well-anchored opinion, my strategy would need a little of Reagan's three-phase communication approach (and perhaps some Sun Tzu).

The campaign's first step would need to follow Reagan's and Sun Tzu's approach and empathize with the public opinion about the neighborhood's challenges, acknowledging that there were tough issues.

Reagan's second step was to reframe the issues from a question of facts to one of feelings. For this, the marketing would have to convert opinion into emotions by comparing our project with others where new development had dramatically improved the neighborhood and increased property values. Then, as with Reagan's approach, I would have to ask if people felt this change was possible in our area.

Using Reagan's third step as a guide, I would have to introduce a powerful new and relevant emotion, fear of loss, and ask how they felt about not buying in those places when prices were incredibly low because the neighborhood was in transition?

The marketing campaign would need to present potential future value and highlight the success of buyers who saw the area as a diamond in the rough. The messaging would need to focus on rewarding early involvement and introduce the fear of loss to evoke emotion so strong it would motivate aggressive action.

It seemed an almost impossible task. I needed to acknowledge the issues. I needed people to believe in the future. I needed to introduce a new emotion. I needed to channel Ronald Reagan. I needed Sun Tzu. I needed a drink.

The big question was how to communicate these messages with such powerful emotion that the audience had no choice but to act. It was a question for which I had no answer—until I heard a flight attendant say, "Welcome aboard."

I'm not a great traveler. On each plane I board, the thought crosses my mind that these folks could be the last people I ever see. So, a pre-dawn flight, sandwiched between my clients en route to visit their development in Mexico, was a surprising time to have an epiphany.

"Please pull out the safety card from the seat pocket in front of you," the attendant said, sounding even less enthused about the flight than her red-eyed passengers.

Holding up the safety card, she flipped it open, as if to show us how to access its information. But I suppose if you need to demonstrate a seatbelt, explaining how to open a pamphlet isn't such a stretch.

"Please pull out the safety card from the seat pocket in front of you" was an announcement made on every flight, every day, to every destination in the world. It's a simple and reasonable request, yet I can't say I've ever seen anyone actually oblige.

Intrigued, I pretended to stretch. Twisting and contorting to see beyond my seat, I surveyed the big Boeing 767. From my spot mid- plane, I could see a few hundred of us squished into neatly organized rows, and not a single person holding the safety card.

A zero percent closing ratio.

I wondered if it had to be like this. What could she say to encourage people to pay attention and act—to get them to reach into that seat pocket and pull out that damn pamphlet?

What emotionally charged language could generate attention and motivate action? It was a question not just for the airline industry, but for every industry, including mine.

Compressed between clients, I began to contemplate the vernacular of motivation. What communication could make something so emotionally compelling it could transform a closing rate from zero to 100 percent?

I imagined the attendant welcoming us on board, smiling warmly and beginning her presentation by describing the last trip's wing-bouncing, aluminum-stretching turbulence, then calmly walking us through the challenge of getting 300+ passengers out of a handful of Hobbit-sized escape hatches before explaining how, in the event of an emergency, the floor aisles would illuminate. (Then adding how this would be of little use if the plane was upside down.)

Once the audience was acutely aware of the risks of their environment, her announcement could detail the flight path over unsearchable mountain ranges and shark-infested oceans. She could explain that crash survival rates increase exponentially with understanding of the safety procedures. Detailed in the pamphlet. Located in the seat pocket. Directly in front of you. That you should pull out and follow along in.

I'm sure the conversion ratio would improve considerably. Yes, the airline would lose every single customer. But that's not the point. My epiphany was about how the power of language could introduce relevant emotion that motivated action, not how to win the customer's hearts and loyalty. (That's in another chapter.)

The choice not to act is grounded by emotional anchors, such as the audience's expectations of a predictable outcome, i.e., landing safely. Emotionally relevant language has the power to enhance motivation and improve conversion ratios dramatically.

Thanks to Sun Tzu, Ronald Reagan and a less-than-energetic flight attendant, I managed to sell out all 1,049 units in the three towers during three opening day events.

Your language is your currency; spend it wisely.

CHAPTER 12

THE MOTIVATION OF EMOTIONAL COMMUNICATION

STEPPING FROM THE CAR INTO THE MIDDAY DESERT SUN, I realized that until that very moment, I'd never experienced real heat. It was so intense that just breathing was a challenge.

Moments earlier, comfy in my air-conditioned SUV, I had wondered how hot the 106 degrees Fahrenheit (41 Celsius for my Canadian friends) that registered on my exterior thermostat actually was.

I stepped towards the fruit stand and stopped. In disbelief, I tried again to fill my lungs, but the sun's heat denied me. With shallow, quick breaths, I headed to the shaded rows of fruit.

In the back, beyond the mounds of big red apples and even bigger, redder tomatoes, sat a pleasant-looking woman attending the till. She smiled as we selected treasures to tide us over on the four hours left of our drive home.

Her two boys, about nine and 11, one on a scooter, the other a skateboard, weaved around the wooden boxes of produce under the shade of the store's awnings. They were close by Mom and just out of the way at the same time.

We dragged our bags of fruit to the front and paid while huge fans kept the woman at the till from overheating. This reminded me that air-conditioned comfort was only a few steps away.

I was about to head to the car when the younger boy popped up and asked, "Would you like to buy a sucker?"

Normally I have all the time in the world for a kid hustling to raise a buck. But at that moment, the sweat was flowing freely and all I could focus on was getting back to that AC. I responded with a discussion-ending, "No, thanks."

This had zero impact.

The boy kept solid eye contact. "We are raising money for a school trip. The suckers are only 50 cents each, and I keep half the money for the trip," he said.

Stuck in his tractor beam, I wasn't leaving without a sucker. Behind him, his mom smiled and gave a small shrug as I dug into my pocket for change and pulled a sucker from its display. Wishing him luck, I again tried to leave.

The boy continued, "The trip is for my entire class. There's a competition to see who can sell the most. So far I am in the lead."

"I don't doubt that for a second," I said, smiling as I turned to go, this time for real.

He continued, "The trip is to Disneyland!" His excitement grew. "AND, if I sell the most suckers, I can bring someone, and I'm going to bring my brother! Would you like to purchase another sucker so you can help me bring my brother to Disneyland?"

"No," I responded, pulling out my wallet. "I won't buy any more suckers, but here is $20 towards your trip for being the best salesperson I have ever met."

Glancing at his mom, I returned her small shrug.

Back in air-conditioned comfort, confident that I had indeed just met the world's best salesperson, I felt relieved to be leaving with my wallet lightened by only $20.50.

During his presentation, I traveled from no to yes, then to buying his product, and eventually to paying more than asking price. All for something I didn't want. It was partly because the kid was so cute, and partly because of heat exhaustion. But regardless of what I bought, what I actually paid for was the experience of an exceptionally staged emotional presentation.

It was a spectacular education, delivered by a nine-year-old, that changed the way I now approach every presentation.

To this day, my sales teams are trained to present segments of information on a predetermined emotional pathway. Each presentation delivers stages of increasing emotion—all of it learned from a scooter-riding sucker salesman moonlighting at a fruit stand.

EMOTIONAL ELEVATION

HOW MANY THINGS HAVE YOU BOUGHT or registered for online this year, be it a book, a course, a subscription or a robo-vacuum?

Most of us have done it multiple times. And in the midst of the process, we often experience at least a small twinge of doubt just as we type in our home address, credit card number and the three-digit security pin on the back of our card.

We hesitate slightly, then with a single click of a final button, our most personal information is whisked into the ether as we shudder to consider who's waiting on the receiving end.

Moments later, we are quietly reassured that things are fine when our email pings, alerting us to the notice confirming our purchase.

While serenity returns with the satisfaction that our sensitive information went to the intended receiver, somehow the clinical confirmation notice on our screen lacks the same level of love we received right up to the point of clicking the "buy now" button. The email arrives and along with it, a slight emotional letdown, right at the worst possible time—a time when even the smallest gesture would have so much meaning.

The challenge is that confirmation emails are something that almost every digital business sends. While it's better than no confirmation, it misses an opportunity to deliver the vital relationship component of **emotional elevation**.

This experience is similar to another one that happens once a year, at least in my house, the unwrapping of the last present on Christmas morning.

The present is opened, appreciated and placed with the other recently revealed gifts. Then in an instant, it hits us all—the excitement that led to Christmas morning is over for another year.

The confirmation email is like that last present. Once you open it, you realize the fun is done. All you have now is a mess to clean up and relatives who won't leave.

Somehow, we're left disappointed. Somehow, this purchasing moment needed to be tempered, not terminated. Somehow, we need emotional elevation.

WHERE'S THE LOVE?

YES, YOU'RE HAPPY TO RECEIVE VERIFICATIOn that it wasn't fraudsters operating a fake magazine subscription sweatshop. But after all the lead-up to your decision, the excitement, the promise of the spectacular—this sad email signals that the emotional euphoria you had when making the decision to buy was temporary. Sigh.

It's a shame. The email senders miss a huge opportunity to fulfill their client's emotional needs, emphasize how much they care, differentiate their company and excite the client about their next purchasing experience.

The good news? It's easy to fix. The great news? There's no better opportunity to achieve so much with so little than immediately after a sale.

Want to build an army of brand ambassadors all focused on telling others how good they feel about your company, product or service? Then get busy using emotional elevation to ease the post-sale fall to reality. Your after-sales engagement, like automated email confirmations, isn't about the confirmation of an order or following up on a sale. It is about securing an emotional connection.

The relationship between seller and buyer is a teeter-totter. Initially, both parties are balanced on a level plane: the seller sells, the buyer buys. During the sales presentation, the seller lifts the buyer emotionally high above them, moving the buyer towards their decision.

But the seller can't hold the buyer emotionally aloft forever. At a certain point, the sale is done and the seller leaves to find another teeter-totter.

Buyers instinctively know that to survive, the sellers must go find other buyers. But they still aren't prepared when the seller steps off the teeter-totter and they plummet from an emotional high, crashing hard.

After the sale, even if the seller fulfills everything that they said they would, the buyer's drop to reality is a letdown. And that is what's remembered.

Regardless of the industry, in order to create a healthy seller-buyer relationship, the seller typically makes big promises and then, if they're good, they keep them.

The delivery of the product and a follow-up ("How's it working out for you?") may seem sufficient. It's not.

Persuaders interested in creating long, loyal and lasting relationships understand that buyers' emotions are most vulnerable the moment a purchase is completed. They know that even the slightest effort at this point will have a greater emotional influence on the buyer's future actions than any other initiative could produce.

Don't get me wrong. Service and follow-up are key contributors to creating happy customers—but only the persuasion of after-sales emotional elevation is strong enough to create an army of brand ambassadors hell-bent on telling everyone how great you are.

The key is to promise big and deliver on that promise, while quietly concealing some small additional benefit to the buyer, then delivering it immediately **after** the sale.

If it's after the sale, the buyer knows the seller didn't have to do it. And because they receive it when their vulnerability is highest, emotional elevation is at its most influential.

Emotional vulnerability is something every seller understands instinctively. But too many use it as an opportunity for short-term gain rather than long-term emotional elevation.

EMOTIONAL ELEVATION:
HOW TO USE IT; HOW NOT TO USE IT

I LEANED FORWARD AND SIGNED THE LAST LINE. I couldn't have been happier; I'd just bought my first new car.

The salesman put the pen back in his pocket, a clear indication we were done. The deal was finished, and my stress started to dissolve.

I don't know about you, but I find buying a car to be a somewhat traumatic ordeal. So, with negotiations over, price agreed to, car care package and personalized options selected, I was relieved.

After a lineage of used automobiles, I would finally be parking a brand new, shiny car in my driveway to emotionally and physically cover the oil-stain reminders of my past vehicles.

Signed and dated—it was all mine.

"Wait, sorry, one last thing," the salesman said.

My stomach tightened.

"I forgot to ask if you want our SDP, Superior Diamond-Tech Glass Protection Against Theft. It lowers your insurance. The package is typically $699 for all windows but you have our car care pack, so you get a discount. On your XL model the discount is even higher, so it's only another six bucks a month based on your payments. Not much for the protection of your $65,000 investment and ... blah blah blah ..." My attention drifted.

My wallet had been metaphorically opened and what the hell, it's a measly few bucks to protect my $65,000 investment. "Sure," I said. "Add it in."

Looking back, I should have known SDP stands for Stupid Dumbass Purchaser. But right then, guard down, wallet open, emotions vulnerable, how could I say no?

Many of you would have told that salesman to shove it in his exhaust pipe, and others may scoff at my falling for this tactic—but be cautious not to judge, for let those who have not fallen for an after-sale upsell be the first to cast a stone. "Would you like to buy our extended warranty?"

It's not the upsell; it's when it was used that's relevant.

With the paperwork finalized, the end in sight, my emotions were as open and unprotected as my wallet. I had little resistance to the request.

Yes, they got another few dollars out of me. But that's not the point. Rather than use the end of our deal as an opportunity to solidify our relationship forever and turn me into their greatest brand ambassador, they used that moment for a financial gain—of six bucks a month. Booo.

The salesman could have said, "Bill, we want to do business with you for a long time. For us, that means earning your business. The cost of the SDP, before discount, is $690. We are going to take care of that for you. I'll have our guys install it right now and I won't charge you for it. It's great. It will lower your insurance and protect your $65,000 investment. We just want you to know how much we appreciate you choosing our dealership over all the others."

Sure, the six bucks a month would probably be hidden in the cost of the vehicle. But this little step, this unnecessary emotional elevation, would have secured me as a brand ambassador for life. The value of which is immeasurable.

It's a great lesson to consider. Leverage emotional vulnerability and make an extra few bucks or exceed expectations and solidify customer loyalty?

There are a huge number of salespeople using after-sales emotion to upsell—and a few emotional revolutionaries who understand its true power and use it to create loyal brand ambassadors.

This is something I experienced at a young age. I can't imagine a childhood anywhere other than the little seaside town where I grew up.

Summers were spent at the beach, across the street from a row of restaurants, ice cream parlors and bathing suit shops.

As our teenage summers hit full stride, the beach remained a big part of our lives and our routine typically included lunch on the strip overlooking the ocean. There was something for every taste, but if you liked fish and chips the choices were endless.

Most of the eateries were walk-up-and-order types. You grabbed your lunch and headed back to eat on the beach while fending off the seagulls.

Summers were packed and those restaurants were always busy, but none busier than Moby Dick Fish and Chips. Run by a local family, the small restaurant always had a massive line of hungry people waiting to order.

Their food was fantastic, but their after-sale emotional elevation was even better.

After enduring the long lineup just to order and pay, you stayed close, ears straining for your number to be called.

Maneuvering through the crowd and back to the pickup counter never led to disappointment. The food arrived with fries overflowing their cardboard containers.

Eyes wide open, hands holding out your ticket, you received your order. Extra fries were piled up like a Jenga tower and on top—no matter how many pieces of fish you ordered—there was always an extra piece thrown in for free.

Their food costs were surely higher than the competitors', but the massive all-day lineups were a strong indication that Moby Dick had figured out emotional elevation.

In the 20-plus years I lived nearby, I never ate at another fish and chips restaurant, and if I had to count, I've probably told five hundred people about that little restaurant. I'm writing about it here now and when I go back to visit the beach, I take my family there every time. I'd say that makes me an ambassador. For the cost of a few fries and an extra piece of cod, it was probably worth it.

My bad experience at the car dealership (and my great experiences at the little beach restaurant) had a strong impact on me. It led me to review my own company's efforts to create brand ambassadors.

I knew our approach was front-loaded but after looking at each part of our process, I was shocked; all our efforts focused on the sale. None focused on creating brand ambassadors.

Yes, we followed up to check on our condo purchasers. But like the waitress asking, "How's the meal?" while your mouth is full of food, we received polite nods and went on our way.

Because my company only marketed new home projects and we continuously sold in different locations, we did little after the sale.

This needed to change. We needed to do better and put more emphasis on after-sales emotional elevation. I started with a small experiment.

Part of the marketing budget was diverted into emotional elevation. Because our homes came with decks and patios, our show suites were equipped with luxurious outdoor furniture and barbecues.

After each sale was finalized, we gave our purchasers a certificate that said that, as a thank you for their business, the developer would have the same barbecue installed on their new deck, free of charge, before they moved in.

Of course, all the purchasers came back to the show suites to check out their new and very unexpected barbecue. This small gesture, delivered as a surprise thank you after the sale, had a huge impact.

Then a strange thing happened. The sales team, experiencing this great excitement, started to let it slip during their presentation that the barbecue was included. The result was the new prospective buyers began asking if we had hidden the cost of the barbecue in the pricing, because not everyone wanted to "pay" for a barbecue. The end result was negative, and the gesture had to be abandoned.

When this unusual addition was presented during the sales presentation it created a negative experience; when it was presented after the sale, it delivered emotional elevation.

Same appliance, different emotion. How strange we humans are.

Not wanting to give up, we adjusted other aspects of our sales process and culture, and that included changing our communication style.

Something I learned about while having my teeth cleaned, believe it or not.

EMOTIONALLY EFFECTIVE COMMUNICATION

THERE'S BEEN A CHANGE AT MY DENTIST.

A typical checkup used to start with the hygienist giving my teeth a good scraping. She'd slip out to fetch the dentist who would waltz in, exchange a few pleasantries and then start rooting around in my mouth.

This routine inevitably included his pained look of disappointment, subtle headshaking and the odd, "Oh, oh." Amidst the scraping and poking of my apparently abysmal teeth, the unpleasant questioning began.

"Do you brush regularly?"

"Do you eat a lot of sugary treats?

And my favorite: "When was the last time you flossed?"

My response, borrowed from a comedian, "How should I know, you did it last?" failed to generate even the smallest smile.

The experience ends with: "There's a lot of work to be done here."

But lately things have changed!

Perhaps it's the fluoride in our water system, or my concentrated efforts to improve dental hygiene, but now I receive nothing but praise during my appointments. My brushing habits have not improved, so I'm guessing it's more likely a result of my dentist attending a seminar on the emotional power of language.

The hard truth is that telling patients they have bad hygiene and bad teeth doesn't encourage them to recommend you or motivate them to rush back for another session of teeth scraping and scolding.

I can imagine the seminar leader. "Try telling your patients they have good dental hygiene; mention that their brushing habits are great. Let them know they have very nice teeth. If they have a cavity, assure them *it is not their fault*. Blame the sugar hidden in our foods, blame the communists, global warming or the government, but whatever you do, compliment them and ensure they feel no responsibility for their issues.

"'Hey, cavities happen. What can you do? It's not your fault. You inherited soft teeth. Now excuse me, the nurse will book you in for next Tuesday. I'm late for my tee time.'"

My dental hygiene hasn't changed over the years, but now I'm constantly reassured that I have a wonderful set of teeth at each appointment. Somehow, through the magic of my dentist's emotional language, I transformed from a chronically inadequate self-health care procrastinator to a miraculously meticulous molar manicurist. My teeth are about the same, but I like my dentist and my dental appointments a lot more.

The approach is effective outside the dentist's office, too. Presenting everything with positive emotional language is always a good idea, even if you are delivering negative information.

"Sorry," my salesman said. "We don't have our floor plans ready to show you yet." Those were the first words I heard walking into my sales center.

After the clients left, I asked, "Why would you say that?"

"Well, we don't have floor plans ready to show people, so I apologize for the inconvenience we caused them."

"Is your apology working?" I asked. "Do they feel better?"

"No," he replied. "People are upset when they hear we aren't ready, and they leave angry."

I thought of my dentist and said, "What about letting people know we are working with the architects to improve the original layouts and provide great living spaces? Explain that the new plans will be finished next week. They're early, but you'd be happy to let them know when the plans are ready."

It was the truth. We had taken over the project from a competitor who hadn't put much thought into the floor plans, so we were changing everything.

The sales team adopted this new language and was amazed at the change in the response.

No longer upset, the visitors to our sales center were now happy that we cared enough to make changes. Our positive language altered attitudes and they now wanted to hear what we had to say. Our number of return visitors increased.

From condos to teeth to whatever you're pitching, keep the language upbeat and emotionally elevating. Your audience will leave happier and return more often.

But you already know this, because you are <u>awesome</u>.

CHAPTER 13

WEAPONS OF MASS ATTRACTION: THE SECRET RECIPE FOR MOTIVATING CROWDS

IN THE DISTANCE I COULD SEE THE EXIT DOORS.

By this point, all the stores, shops and aisles in the mall had blended into one big confusing spiteful maze.

I have an aversion to shopping and an even stronger dislike of malls. So, like a mouse spotting the cheese, I picked up the pace and headed for the doors. Making one last left turn, I ran directly into a wall of people.

No one budged. Now, I was angry.

"Why the hell would you stand right in the middle of the aisle?! What's wrong with you people …" My mental rant paused as, like everyone else, I stared at the spectacle in front of me.

Like ants on a picnic blanket, a dozen people crawled all over stacks of rugs. Pulling, grabbing, throwing the unwanted aside. Dragging out a rug, then vaulting back for another. Chaos.

I asked another shopper what was happening. Without moving her eyes from the madness, she pointed to a small sign.

More joined the scrum and I wondered, "How cheap can these rugs be to make people act like this?"

Curiosity overpowered embarrassment. Inching towards the frenzy, I cautiously lifted the corner of a small round foyer rug. $260. I struggled with the math. Sixty percent off. That meant—today only—it was 104 bucks!

"You taking that one?" A lady interrupted my thoughts.

"No, it's okay, I was just …," I began to say, as the rug disappeared.

I stepped towards the large area rugs and flipped a corner, then a second, and a third—incredible! The big rugs were all priced the same as the small ones. Every rug was $104!

And just like that, I was elbow-to-elbow, grabbing, flipping and dragging. When the madness stopped, covered in lint and dust, I stared at my pile. This was the deal of the century!

At home, I triumphantly unrolled my treasures. My girlfriend's only response: "Why rugs? We have wall-to-wall carpeting, like, in every room."

A point I hadn't considered.

"There was this huge sale … I was lucky to … there were so many people …"

My explanation stalled as she walked from the room.

Alone with my rugs, floating atop a sea of already carpeted floors, I questioned my sanity.

Why would a sane person, crushed by the weight of a new mortgage, buy rugs to put on top of other rugs? What was I thinking?

I had no need for rugs, but somehow I'd lost my sh!t and now owned hundreds of dollars' worth of area rugs I had no use for.

How did this happen?

Damn you, "60% Off."

Damn you, "Today Only."

Damn you, frenzied crowd.

I never stopped to think of costs or mortgages or my wall-to-wall carpeted home or my girlfriend, who lacked interior design vision. I never thought at all. My actions were 100 percent emotion driven. I was snatched from independent thought and pushed into irrational action by the perfect recipe of cognitively enticing ingredients. Everything combined to alert my attention, engage my emotion, separate me from common sense and ultimately manipulate my actions.

I needed to understand this incredible recipe, but first I had to break down the ingredients.

THE SEVEN INGREDIENTS OF EMOTIONAL INFLUENCE

1. INCONGRUENT INTERRUPTION (INITIAL DISRUPTION)

A lot has been written on the power of permission-based marketing. Fantastic stuff, but before you can ask for permission you need to interrupt the right people, at the right time, in the right place. And to accomplish disruption, your presentation needs to be, well, odd.

Call it what you like—interruptive, disruptive, disturbance or distraction, whether it's print, digital, traditional, guerrilla, outdoor, in-store, in-house or outhouse—the first ingredient is to evoke interest by stepping into your audience's path and interrupting them with an incongruity.

In my mall encounter, the behavior of the group standing in the aisle was irregular. This alerted my subconscious to a potential threat or the possibility of reward. This is the first step in attention disruption, but it goes deeper than that. Let me explain.

Because our minds constantly search for threat and reward, initial interruption is an imperative element that forces our subconscious to stop, understand and predict a consequence. Once the attention-interruption is processed, if it doesn't link to a purpose, we set it aside and quickly move on to deal with the next disruption.

So, if you're going to interrupt someone, the best way to do so is to be different. But if you are going to be different, you'd better connect your difference to your purpose—or your attention-intrusion is wasted.

Being different just to be different may grab your audience's attention, but without purpose, you won't hold it.

When incongruent interruption is connected to a purpose, it converts to message acceptance.

For example, an image of a cow standing upright on the back of another cow while spray-painting graffiti on a billboard that says "*eat mor chickin*" interrupts our attention.

Clever. We realize the ad's purpose is to present cows encouraging us to eat more chicken. The cognitive processing supports the incongruent visual and connects its purpose to the Chick-fil-A chicken restaurant's message.

If the cognitive processing evoked is too simple, however, the message may be too easily dismissed.

A Red Bull commercial featuring a boy giving pigs the energy drink to create a "when pigs fly" scenario illustrates this issue. The imagery is too obvious, and the viewer doesn't need to work out the connection. As such, there is no reward for effort, no "aha" moment, and the advertisement is forgotten as quickly as it was viewed.

But let's say you used flying pigs to advertise bacon-flavored chicken wings. This imagery would not only trigger deep cognitive processing, connect the visual to a purpose, and ultimately provide a reward for decrypting the message connection—it would also represent one of the greatest new food inventions on this Earth.

2. SUBCONSCIOUS ENGAGEMENT (SECONDARY SUPPORT)

The wall of collectively mesmerized shoppers was the incongruent interrupter that triggered my cognitive processing—witnessing the erratic behavior of the Mount Rug climbers was the subconscious engagement that connected the interruption with a purpose.

My attention in the mall was definitely interrupted, but my interest intensified when I subconsciously connected the interruption (the actions of the people in the aisle) and the visual of the crazed shoppers climbing on the rugs.

When you smell smoke, you're intrigued. But if you smell smoke and see people running, your actions are intensified.

3. DISRUPTION OF PERCEIVED VALUE (ALTER PREEXISTING BELIEFS)

When enticing an audience, it's critical to consider their existing beliefs and perceptions of value. It is a step the best persuaders don't miss, and the final component before influencing motivation.

Wow, all these people are grabbing rugs!

*Maybe it's the **60% OFF**.*

I wonder how this % relates to my perception of value …

My attention interrupted, the erratic behavior of others subconsciously supporting and intensifying my interest, the ***60% OFF*** sign intrigued my perception of value.

Are these rugs really a good deal? Is this why everyone is acting irregularly?

Flipping over the small rug, my perception of value was intrigued by the sale price. It represented great value. But my perception was disrupted, not shattered.

If I'd been in the market for rugs, I would have acted based on this point alone. The point here is that any relevant ad placed in front of an already converted audience looking specifically for what you're selling will achieve some effect. (But this is a needle in a haystack approach.) My only desire was to get out of that damn mall, and I was not at all interested in buying rugs—until the introduction of a perception disrupter.

4. THE PERCEPTION DISRUPTER (ESTABLISH <u>NEW</u> PERCEPTION OF VALUE)

You have seen these before…

Wait! If you act now, we'll send you a second set of Ginsu Knives absolutely free!

I don't want any more kitchen knives, but a second set for free! WOW!

Wait? The large rugs are the same price as the small rugs. What!?

Creating unrelated value between similar offerings influences our perception of value, like adding a second set of knives or offering a low-cost, first-class seat upgrade at the check-in counter or pricing a stack of large rugs at the same price as the small ones.

Without the influence of emotion, we determine value through comparative processing. But when we have little to compare (i.e., a single stack of rugs) the process is challenging until a relevant comparable is added—like another stack of rugs.

In his book *Predictably Irrational*, behavioral economist Dan Ariely describes how our comparative analysis processing can be influenced. Ariely explains that when facing several slightly different options, if two are similar but one of those two offers marginally higher value, these two easily comparable options will sway all attention from the other choices.

When I flipped over the large rugs and saw the pricing, my existing perception of value was shattered by comparative processing and suddenly, like Elvis, my rationale had left the building. A new emotion arrived, as fear of loss became the emotional motivator.

5. THE EMOTIONAL MOTIVATOR (HUMAN COMPETITION INSTINCT)

With value disrupted and a new value perceived, my desires were activated and the object became the reward. The actions of the other shoppers on the rug piles elevated my emotional fear of loss and intensified my actions.

We've seen it in almost every industry.

"The auction is closing in seven minutes—bid now or lose out."

Human competition intensifies fear of loss and becomes an emotional motivator at an instinctual level. Now, aided by evolution-driven adrenaline, my actions grew more urgent as I focused on avoiding loss, not just acquiring reward. I needed not just one rug, but lots of rugs.

In short, I began to act because of and like everyone else.

6. CONVERSION TO CROWD MENTALITY (LOSS OF INDIVIDUAL THOUGHT)

"All these people can't be wrong."

Competition causes the abandonment of individual thought and assimilation of the crowd's mentality.

When interruption becomes subconscious engagement, altering perceived value, and fear of loss ignites competition—the result is cognitive disconnection.

A crowd's energy is consuming. Just watch the lineups at a Boxing Day Sale or Black Friday event, where even the most rational thinkers soon trade their common sense for crowd-sense.

When there is competition for something we desire, our motivation for ownership and perception of its value are influenced by the actions of others.

Ask a 13-year-old why he absolutely must have a specific style of $400 running shoes (despite the fact that his growth rate means those "beauty kicks" will spend less time on his feet than it took Mom and Dad to earn them).

In the same way the first bidder establishes demand at an auction, competition has the power to make an audience trust the crowd's perception of value over their own.

With reward in hand, fear of loss is replaced by rich emotional satisfaction.

7. THE EMOTIONAL REWARD (EXPERIENCE)

The greater the struggle, the more importance we place on gaining the reward and the higher our perceived value of it becomes.

Everyone wanted these. It was crazy, people tugging, pulling, grabbing, fuzz flying! But I picked the best ones—I'm leaving with six incredible rugs.

What began as incongruent interruption ended with emotional reward. Like bookends, these two components hold up the emotional elements that influence our actions.

My "rug-apalooza" may have been caused by coincidentally aligned components, but these elements can be replicated anywhere to create weapons of mass attraction. And persuaders do it all the time.

To understand how persuaders use these combinations and techniques to manipulate, it's important to first understand how humans receive incoming stimuli and how our cognitive processing works.

COGNITIVE PROCESSING

Is this a threat, or a reward?

EVER MET SOMEONE FOR THE FIRST TIME, eyed them up and down, noticed their outfit, shoes, handshake, haircut? What is it you're really looking for? Overall appearance, social clues, body language—anything that will determine if they represent potential threat or possible reward. Studies have revealed that we judge out of instinct. We do it fast. And we do it to survive.

Humans can accurately judge disingenuousness, honesty and trustworthy character traits within seconds. Harvard scientist Amy Cuddy explains that our instinctive need to protect ourselves is deeply connected to our survival. We naturally judge in order to keep ourselves safe.

The accuracy of these first impressions is a subject of experiments that have been ongoing for over 20 years.

In a study completed at Northeastern University, researchers Dana Carney, Randall Colvin and Judith Hall found that our first impressions tell us a lot, and some characteristics are discernable within just five seconds. These studies show that the rate of accuracy doesn't improve even when the time frame is extended to five minutes.

Additional research demonstrates that we can also accurately assess situations and predict outcomes within seconds. Psychology student

Tricia Prickett at Oregon State University showed a collection of video-taped job interviews and found that observers could accurately predict the outcome of the interview after watching only the first 15 seconds.

Two hours of typing a résumé for a 15-second job interview? Sounds about right.

Our ability to assess a situation with very limited information was first referred to as "thin slicing" in 1992 by psychologists Nalini Ambady and Robert Rosenthal. (It was also the subject of Malcolm Gladwell's 2005 book *Blink: The Power of Thinking Without Thinking*.) The thin-slicing concept suggests that we have evolution-enhanced prediction capabilities and our instincts are often as accurate as predictions that are well researched. It turns out we can judge a book by its cover.

Once formulated, we tightly hold (and defend) our assumptions. These help us avoid time-consuming cognitive processing of possible outcomes in everyday situations, such as "Will each step hold my weight as I walk down these stairs?"

But our instinctive judgments mean that we filter everything through predetermined beliefs, and contradictory information is dismissed.

When you're trying to communicate new information, such as marketing a new product as superior or presenting contradictory evidence, the audience filters your messages through their preset prejudices, beliefs and opinions.

As I've mentioned throughout this book, motivating an audience's desire to change by presenting features, facts and details is met with strong resistance.

If you've always preferred the Ford brand, say, then marketing from the competing Chevrolet brand that presents their quality as superior is processed through your preset beliefs and ultimately dismissed. Now not only are Chevys inferior, but their makers can't even be trusted to tell you the truth.

This contributes to why we typically don't tend to stray from a brand or product.

I'm a Boston Bruins fan. As a kid, I worshipped their legendary players Phil Esposito and Bobby Orr. Now, aside from the team crest and colors, pretty much everything I loved about the team has changed. Espo and Orr haven't played for the Bruins in 45 years. Coaches, players, management—even the stadium, the old Boston Gardens—are all gone.

Logic would say I should find a new team, because the things that originally connected me have changed. But I'm still a Bruins fan. Whether it's a brand, product or a sports team, it's not the facts that anchor us. It's the emotion, and that is anchored in our instinctual drive to survive.

Combine our instinctive thin-slicing evaluation process with the way we filter new information through predetermined beliefs, and marketing has a tough challenge.

How many seconds do you give new flyers or direct mail envelopes before they get tossed into the recycle bin?

To change an audience's opinion, you must unhook their emotional anchors, which means competing against evolution. But first you must get their attention, a tough obstacle given the amount of incoming information we receive.

This is why we pay attention to the abnormal and incongruent.

It is also how we process, of all things, humor—and why marketing so often relies on comedy to present its message.

KNOCK, KNOCK:
WHY DO HUMANS REACT TO HUMOR?

PERHAPS A KNOCK-KNOCK JOKE didn't compel our ancestors to migrate off the grassy plains of the savanna—but the cognitive patterns they used to assess threats and rewards are the same we use when processing a joke.

If humor is incongruent and unexpected, it receives priority; if it is also relevant, then we pay attention to it.

Cavemen sit around a fire debating where best to find a mate. One suggests that, tonight, they all go out clubbing.

Just as thin-slicing makes it possible to evaluate and find patterns in situations and behavior, similar cognitive processing occurs when we try to interpret humorous information or situations. It's a search for a satisfactory resolution of uncertainty.

We process humor by isolating the unexpected from the predictable. We then work on decoding the information to determine a probable resolution. This decoding process creates a longer mental shelf life, keeping humor (and marketing) in focus for longer.

It's important to understand that—whether it is in marketing or in humor—the audience will dismiss the message if they see it as predictable or irrelevant. Knock, knock. Who's there? Smell mop …

That joke has zero relevance, unless you have a four-year-old; then you are committing it to memory right now.

In the movie *Daddy's Home Two,* John Lithgow plays an ultra-cheerful, affectionate grandfather whose cute jokes make his grandchildren giggle.

Mel Gibson plays a contrasting "rough around the edges" grandfather. Unfamiliar with children, he attempts to endear himself to his grandkids with his own humor: "Two dead hookers wash up onshore …" but is stopped mid-joke by the horrified parents of the wide-eyed children.

For the family, Gibson's joke wasn't relevant and therefore it wasn't considered funny. But the audience in the movie theater found relevance and humor in Gibson's misguided attempt to impress the children.

The movie audience processed the incongruent (unexpected) information against what they understood about the situation. The scene held the viewer's attention by presenting an example of Gibson's character as an unfit grandfather. Ultimately, the audience reaction was laughter.

Like humor, if marketing is incongruent yet relevant, we are hardwired to pay attention and decipher its meaning. Because our instincts demand we predict the outcome (message or punch line), we work to resolve the uncertainty and understand the information received.

INCONGRUITY, INTERPRETATION AND RESOLUTION

IN HUMOR, THIS COMBINATION CAUSES LAUGHTER. In marketing, it creates message adhesiveness—that is, communication that sticks.

One of the earliest and most effective examples of incongruity, interpretation and uncertainty resolution was the 1925 Burma-Vita Company campaign to introduce its Burma-Shave brushless shaving cream.

The marketing elevated their new product from virtual obscurity to the second highest-selling shaving cream in the U.S.

Burma-Shave signs were spaced out on long stretches of open highway. Each sign communicated one segment of a sequential message for passing motorists to read, interpret and resolve.

DOES YOUR HUSBAND

Typically presented in sets of six, the signs were designed with a single-color background and easy-to-read font. The advertising messages were placed far enough apart that motorists had time to think about each one and connect it with the previous sign before seeing the next.

MISBEHAVE

The mechanics of this approach generated cognitive processing of each sign and secured engagement until the audience was rewarded with the satisfaction and resolution of the full message.

GRUNT AND GRUMBLE

The Burma-Shave message lasted long after the narrative concluded. (It is interesting to note that in 1956, Princeton University cognitive psychologist George Miller published a paper explaining that at any given time, the average person can only hold about seven items in their short-term memory.)

RANT AND RAVE?

We have evolved to interpret incoming data instantaneously—today, our unconscious mind works overtime to keep pace with the massive volume of interruptive advertising we need to process.

SHOOT THE BRUTE

Consider how quickly you decide to read beyond a headline or pay attention to an online advertisement.

SOME BURMA-SHAVE!

In the hunt for traction, too many marketers try to achieve message effectiveness without engaging our instinctive processing. They simply throw what they can where they can, hoping for something to stick. The result is audience indifference.

One notable exception to this is the Government Employees' Insurance Company of Texas. After years of failing to reach their market effectively, they decided to change direction. Their marketing team dropped the details and used incongruent yet relevant humor to make their company more human and to connect emotionally across a national platform.

Now better known as Geico, the company spends close to a billion dollars a year on advertising featuring their little green British-accented gecko.

Geico's chairman, Warren Buffett, the "world's wealthiest elder," acquired 100 percent control of the company in 1995, and has said he would spend two billion a year on advertising if he could.

The Geico gecko, a brainchild of the Martin Agency, was created out of necessity during the 1999 Screen Actors Guild strike. Actors weren't available. The friendly little gecko was given an unexpected British accent and has gone on to appear in over 145 different commercials.

In 2005, the company's humanized gecko was listed by the American Association of Advertising Agencies as one of the top advertising icons in America—and they paid a hefty price to get there!

Geico's marketing team combined relevant emotional creativity with big budgets. The aggressive budgets combined their beneficial message of cheaper insurance and the incongruity of an anthropomorphically animated lizard (sorry, gecko) with a cockney accent.

Using humor to deliver your marketing message is a great way to create adhesiveness, as long as either your approach is relevant—that is, connecting your message to your purpose—or you have the luxury of massive budgets.

There have never been as many communication avenues available as there are today. Yet it has never been harder to access and hold attention.

With more and more advertising platforms available, the human adaptive unconscious is working harder to define what deserves attention. Alongside that process, our resolve to ignore the marketing barrage strengthens.

To rise above the competing noise and gain attention control, the best persuaders rely on a combination of ingredients.

The seven core emotional ingredients of successful persuasion:

1. **RELEVANCE**

   Understand your audience's interests and present within them.

2. **INCONGRUENT DISRUPTION**

   Interrupt with incongruencies to generate initial interest.

3. **PURPOSEFUL DIFFERENTIATOR**

   Connect your difference to your purpose (the Geico gecko).
   Being different for the sake of being different is ineffective.

4. **EMOTIONAL COMMUNICATIONS**

   Connect your product, service or brand to your audience's emotions.

5. **EVOKE COGNITIVE PROCESS**

   Trigger the audience's instinctive need to decode your information and uncover the meaning of your message.

6. **INTRODUCE FEAR OF LOSS**

   From inclusion to exclusion, from limited availability to restricted access, create the fear of missing out. Introduce a relevant devil.

7. **REWARD FOR ACTION**

   Deliver emotionally beneficial rewards connected to your audience's decision to act.

The first step, obviously, is to initiate interest. Without this, influence is impossible. Whether it's through abrupt interruption (a negative headline) or an incongruent enticement (the Burma-Shave signs or an image of cows painting a billboard), the objective is to capture attention by sparking your audience's curiosity.

With curiosity secured, the next objective is to trigger cognitive processing and start your audience connecting your message with your purpose—well before you request their action.

Too many campaigns miss this key middle step (cognitive processing) and jump from interruption immediately into call to action.

Only ~~9~~ 8 left!

Hurry! Call today!

This approach finds its way into advertising all too often. Typically starting with the presentation of a fact, such as decreasing availability, it fails to present incongruity, entice interest or encourage cognitive processing. With no interest or emotion evoked and no cognitive processing required, the audience is left with dismissible facts: There were nine—now there are eight. So what?

There is no component of relevance or differentiation, so there is no need to process. Without these elements, fear of loss has no power as a call to action.

Remember Mountain Dew's CGI mascot, Puppy Monkey Baby? If you're lucky, this terrifying hybrid has escaped your recollection.

Its incongruent disruption had a varied effect on the 100 million-plus 2016 Super Bowl audience when it aired. The ad definitely enticed the viewer's cognitive process. And it created an emotion—even if that emotion was disgust for some. The ad did its job.

The soft drink company attributes their strong increase in sales to Puppy Monkey Baby. Regardless of how horrific chubby baby legs attached to a furry monkey body with the head of a pug puppy may be to those of us 30 years or older—to the mid-teen, energy-drink-pounding male target audience, the image was relevant and evoked cognitive processing.

The key is to understand what's relevant to your audience. Miss it and they'll swipe, flip, scroll and otherwise move on to the next round of message bombardment headed their way. But deliver a relevant interruption that activates your audience's interest and alerts their instincts—and you'll override their barriers to action.

PULLING IT ALL TOGETHER— ACTION OR AWARENESS?

ONE COMPANY THAT USED THESE ELEMENTS to create a mascot (avoiding the cringe factor of Mountain Dew's mammal crossbreeding) is the American Family Life Assurance Company. This large and relatively characterless insurance corporation's quest for connection led them to a duck.

The American Family Life Assurance Company, affectionately known as Aflac, used its wing-flapping, vocabulary-challenged spokes-duck to frantically quack in frustration when confronted with the question of who to contact for better insurance benefits.

But was it as easy as introducing a quacking duck?

For the 10 years prior to their now famous duck campaign, Aflac focused on promoting name recognition through an array of advertising. Nothing worked and they struggled to achieve even 10-percent name recognition across North America.

In the 10 years following the introduction of the duck, Aflac reported 94-percent national name recognition. According to a 2009 interview with Aflac's CEO Dan Amos, their sales doubled in the three years following the launch of the duck campaigns.

The incongruence of a quacking duck in an insurance ad evoked their audience's cogitative processing and connected with their product, using humor to achieve message adhesiveness.

Aflac's little white duck quacked its way to top-of-mind (and top of heart, but more on that later) to achieve iconic status.

Using relevant, incongruent imagery transports your audience into consideration of your message. When you include a connection between product and purpose—your message sticks.

Unless your audience is thinking about your message beyond the moment it gained their attention, the core purpose—generating action— will fall short.

It's about more than just attaining attention—once you have it, you need to hold it and direct it. Ever been interrupted by an advertisement that struck you as odd or interesting, yet moments later, you can't recall the product? If the initial presentation achieves audience interruption yet fails to activate cognitive processing—the result is often millions spent, millions watched, and zero results.

This underwhelming return on advertising isn't a rarity. A great number of brands advertise, not with the intention of delivering an adhesive message, but for the sole purpose of achieving brand awareness.

While it is true that most consumers spend mere seconds scanning the shelves before reaching for the familiar, this focus on visibility to achieve emotionless top-of-mind awareness leaves the presenters vulnerable to the next competitor with bigger budgets.

This marketing budget misfire disregards the power of persuasion and is a wasted opportunity to achieve more than just half a minute of mindshare.

COMPETING FOR TOP OF MIND

EVEN IF YOU EVOKE HUMAN COGNITIVE PATTERNS and generate interest, how can anyone with limited resources be successful when facing today's billion-dollar corporate budgets?

For that answer, we need to go back about 2,500 years and again take a page or two from Sun Tzu's book.

In the sixth century B.C., the Chinese general and military strategist wrote *The Art of War*. His theme? Use what you have. If you are small, be nimble. If you are big, be aggressive.

Sun Tzu's point was that you must understand your assets and your enemy's assets. Then fight on your terms, not theirs.

The advice holds true today. When up against a well-armed opposition with Goliath-sized budgets, your ability to be creatively nimble means a well-aimed message can defeat a big-budget-wielding giant.

Sun Tzu believed the great equalizer was creativity, and David used it to knock out his behemoth competitor. But in today's economy, is it really possible to compete against giants with seemingly unlimited marketing spend and infinite reach?

Yes. Yes, it is.

The secret is that big money doesn't equate to big influence any more than wealth guarantees good taste.

Too frequently, the bigger the budget, the stronger the belief that bombardment equates to effectiveness. Those piloting these advertising barrages often place more emphasis on the influence of their impact rather than the impact of their influence.

This is based on the belief that market share and mindshare are exclusively connected.

That belief is wrong.

Yes, pounding away at the minds of millions can lead to top-of-mind awareness and market share, as long as budgets keep growing and the competition doesn't aim for your audience's heart.

Even the smallest budgets can excel by focusing on something more effective than market share or mindshare.

WHAT'S BETTER THAN TOP OF MIND?

"Exposure! Consistent repetition! You must own top of mind to have market share! The minute a client doesn't see you, you're gone forever!"
–Advertising sales reps, everywhere–

BUT IS MINDSHARE LINKED DIRECTLY TO MARKET SHARE? If not, then what is?

Nestled beside our kitchen phone sits a notepad. (Yes, we still have a landline. How else would I partake in those important personal surveys from call centers in India?) It's a nice lined notepad, generously delivered through our mail slot by a local realtor. And three feet away, on the side of our fridge, is a different agent's smiling photo atop the calendar he drops by each year.

These guys never miss a seasonal reason to send us stuff. Each October a pumpkin is on our porch, in December it's a Christmas tree, every Canada Day the boulevard is lined with cute little flags. No season? No problem, their "Just Sold!" flyers and appetizing recipes printed on glossy postcards arrive with regularity.

These guys have exposure. They have regularity. They have top-of-mind awareness, consistent messaging and repetition.

Somewhere a delivery company, a printer and a pumpkin farmer rejoice.

Everybody knows them. These successful realtors have definitely earned top of mind. Ask people in the neighborhood (I have) who they think of first, and these realtors' names come up every time.

When I sell my house, while the guilt pangs as I write my to-do lists on their[2] notepads and my kids' hockey schedule on their calendars, I won't list my house with either of them.

Regardless of their mindshare, consistent exposure, notepads and Bumble Pie recipe cards, I'll use another realtor. I met her working at open houses, I trust her, our family likes her, and while she doesn't deliver Easter eggs or pumpkins, she does have something else of a much greater value—**heartshare**.

MINDSHARE = MARKET SHARE?

THE REAL QUESTION IS, what influences choice? Do we choose one fast-food chain over another—because, as McDonald's claims, "I'm lovin' it"? Or do we buy their burgers[3] because of their mindshare? Do we actually love it? Or have we been bombarded into "Lovin' it"?

Those who consider mindshare to be the determining factor in consumer choice continue to seek increased exposure. The consequences of this circular reasoning lead many to escalate their spending in search of "more eyeballs." But this quest for exposure leaves them, well, exposed.

Mindshare influences choice but it's as expensive to maintain as it is risky to rely on. Too often, an audience influenced by mindshare alone can be easily enticed by competitors with bigger budgets or better features.

---

2 **Full Confession:** I hope the realtors don't read this and cut me off. Those notepads are really handy.

3 Once every two years something clicks and I think, "Ya know, a Big Mac right now would be perfect." Then, two years later, about the time it takes to forget how I felt after eating that hamburger last time, I think, "Ya know, a Big Mac right now would be perfect …."

MINDSHARE OVER MATTER

WITHOUT EMOTIONAL INFLUENCE, choice is often based on what we are exposed to the most.

To the audience, some choices seem better, some worse, but most seem more or less the same. Rarely will one option rise head and shoulders above the rest based on its own merit. With no standout preference, choice becomes a default decision based upon who has mindshare at the moment.

This has led many to believe that repetition has absolute power. If mindshare hunters grasped the true nature of influence, they'd realize that mindshare is temporary, and always available to the highest bidder.

Persuaders understand that true influence comes from heartshare, not mindshare or massive repetition and exposure. But before we discuss this, let me ask, can you finish this jingle? "There's two scoops of raisins in a package of ..."

Even if you haven't read the first half of this book, you'll recognize the famous Raisin Bran pitch that Kellogg's has used since the 1960s.

If your memory is exceptional, you'll recall their advertising ditties about the lumberjack, "Sturdy Dan McGee, who was up his 59th tree" but climbed down just for a bowl of Raisin Bran; and the young BMX racer who gave up being in first place to pedal over for a bowl. "More than bikes, what Danny likes is two scoops of raisins."

It seems that raisins have the power to pull adults off trees and kids from bike races (especially those named Daniel). With two scoops worth of this magical ingredient, Kellogg's sells about 38 million boxes of Raisin Bran each year, but is it really their abundance of raisins that motivates our action? Or is it the exposure and repetition that's convinced us to look beyond the fact that a "scoop" is not a standard unit of measurement? If we were counting, the actual volume, according to *The Science*

Creative Quarterly, is about 1¼ cups of raisons in a 20-ounce box, which seems a tad different than the two heaping scoops held by the package's smiley sun caricature. But I digress.

The point is, regardless of the raisin-to-flake ratio, the two scoops feature has become a pillar of the audience's default decision. And that's Kellogg's Achilles heel.

I'm in the cereal aisle. I recognize Kellogg's, I enjoy their products, I grab a box. Hey, like the song says, every package has two scoops of raisins. But their marketing and repetitious jingle connect this default decision to a feature, not an emotion. And features can be bested, while emotions can't.

"Two scoops of raisons" may sell a lot of breakfast cereal, but what happens when a competitor adds a third scoop? As a fruit and bran fan, would you at least try a box? What if the taste was similar, and the cereal had way more raisins? What if the price was lower and this new brand supported their campaign with taste tests and raisin counts, had their own jingle ("Three scoops a box!") and maybe even included a secret toy. Would you go back to Kellogg's? And, just like that, a new competitor decimates the benefits of 40+ years of worth of raisin bran-ding.

It's the ever-present danger that all brands built on function, features or price have to face every single day and support with constantly expanding budgets.

It's something that brands built on emotion don't have to worry about—because emotion is more powerful than facts and features.

Default decisions do not equate to customer loyalty. They are based on familiarity and habit, something that can be broken and tossed aside should a competitor offer better facts, functionality or lower prices.

It's amazing how many big brands watch in wonder as competitors out-feature or underprice them to gain market share, taking away customers en masse. The typical big brand's response? Escalate spending to increase exposure in an effort to recapture mindshare.

They simply don't understand the emotional power of heartshare. If they did, they'd fight back by aiming at their audience's heart rather than their head. Budgets could be slashed; profits would explode, and ultimately, market share would be secured.

But what is heartshare, how does it work, and how do you gain it?

THE VALUE OF HEARTSHARE

IT'S RARE TO SEE A PORSCHE ADVERTISEMENT. They exist, but you have to look hard to find one. When you do, their approach is clear. They focus on heartshare (not mindshare) and creating an emotional connection between their product and their audience.

Rather than babble on about performance, engineering and design (and they most certainly could), Porsche connects their brand with the audience's emotions and memories, not their heads.

Their ads reach into our earliest memories. They connect emotionally with the heart and leave the brain out of the equation.

In one of their famously hard-to-find ads, the headline evokes emotion by simply asking, "Honestly now, did you spend your youth dreaming about someday owning a Nissan or a Mitsubishi?"

Porsche gets it. They understand that access to the buyer's wallet is through the heart, not the head. More importantly, they understand the difference between **connecting emotionally** and **presenting emotionally**.

This subtlety is the distinction between temporarily capturing an audience's mindshare versus connecting with an audience using heartshare.

A recent Chrysler TV commercial introduced the new Jeep Cherokee.

Images of pristine wilderness, sunlit caverns and desert landscapes contrast with cloud-shrouded mountains as the Cherokee drives seamlessly from suburban streets to mist-covered roads lit by distant lightning strikes.

The stark visual contrasts present strong imagery and the voice-over smoothly describes the Jeep, in calm, single-phrase articulation.

"Captivating exteriors. Dynamic lighting. Elevated comfort. Powerfully efficient.

One more thing. The world comes with it."

The images are overlaid with words like NEW, BOLDER LOOK, PREMIUM LED HEADLAMPS, NAPPA LEATHER-TRIMMED SEATS.

It's all choreographed to the emotionally empowering Fleetwood Mac song "Go Your Own Way," concluding with the tagline: "The Reimagined 2019 Cherokee."

Nice try. But by putting way too much focus on features, they missed the magic.

Imagine if the Chrysler Corporation took a different approach, forgot about the features and embraced the emotions? What if they leveraged emotion to tackle social challenges and tried to bring the world together—rather than sell their Jeeps using lightning strikes and distant thunder? Could they possibly encourage human harmony and connect it with their product, their history and their own struggles as a company and as individuals?

It's a tall order, but at least worthy of an effort. Perhaps they could try by generating a campaign something like the one that follows.

MORGAN FREEMAN NARRATES, his tone and tempo reminiscent of his voice in *The Shawshank Redemption*.

The ad is an emotional statement about how we are at our strongest when we come together. The underlying message is that many forces are focused on separating us, creating conflict to drive us apart, make us weaker, divide us and conquer us. Some are natural and some are human, but we succeed and persevere if we work together.

Times are tough

Video footage: Unemployment signs, CLOSED signs, food bank lineups

"Fires. Floods. Tension."

Video footage: Riots, fires, local and international conflicts

"We all feel it. The world is hurting."

Video footage: Nurses' faces; COVID-19 hospital scene

"It's easy to close in, detach."

Video footage: Elderly lady looking out care home window.

"Now, more than ever, we need to remember how great we are…"

Video footage: Young white man stands up, motions to an older black woman, offering his seat on the bus.

"…when we work together, we can achieve anything."

Video footage: Flood victim relief supplies are unloaded from a Jeep.

"It's when we learned who we really are…."

Video footage: WW2 women working in ammunition plants.

"…and the ability of the human spirit to endure."

Video footage: Eisenhower riding in a Jeep, Second World War.

"Chrysler believes in this human spirit…"

Video footage: Black and white images of factory workers on assembly line.

"…we know our strongest moments have come by working together."

Video footage: Soldiers liberating town, being kissed by civilian girls.

"It's how we learned who we really are…"

Video footage: Newspaper victory headline; WW2 celebrations

"…as a company and as citizens of the world, we owe everything to working together."

Video footage: WW2 celebrations

"Chrysler. We support those who believe in perseverance."

Video footage: An exhausted doctor walks towards a Jeep. It's dark, and there is no one else around.

"We will get through this. Like we've always said, tough times don't last but tough people do."

Video footage: Doctor drives his Jeep into his driveway.

"Together we are better. Together we will overcome. Together we can do anything."

Video footage: Doctor walks into his home. His wife, waiting for him on the couch, looks up at him and smiles warmly.

"Chrysler. Drive together."

With sufficient advertising, messaging and branding, big spenders can create mindshare. But without heartshare, even the most recognizable companies are vulnerable to competitors wielding bigger budgets, or an even more dangerous weapon: Price.

TOP OF MIND DOESN'T MEAN TOP OF WALLET

CONSIDER THE MINDSHARE LEADER GILLETTE.

After buying its shaving products for generations, Gillette's lifelong customers headed en masse to the competition.

It seems Gillette's matrix for customer loyalty was transaction activity, and they over-calculated the value of their mindshare.

For years, their customers, untethered by heartshare, were actually relying on a default decision; they selected Gillette based on the brand's familiarity and visibility.

With no emotional connection, the audience considered the Gillette products to be similar to those of the competition. Out of habit, given no reason to change, consumers stayed true to the brand. That is, until new competitors entering Gillette's market space presented much less expensive alternatives—and Gillette customers realized just how long they'd been suffering from razor burn.

A *Wall Street Journal* 2017 headline stated: **"Gillette, Bleeding Market Share, Cuts Prices of Razors.** Top brand also plans to add focus on its cheaper products as pressure mounts from online start-ups."

The article explained how Gillette had dominated the global razor business using their longtime strategy of adding features, then raising prices. (Why use a three-blade razor when you can shave with a five blade "Fusion" razor instead?!) But their strategy was losing ground.

In response to competitive pressures and shrinking market share, the 115-year-old Gillette Corporation[4] adjusted their strategy. They stopped adding features and shaved prices instead.

According to the *Wall Street Journal*, Gillette's spokesperson said of the decision to reduce pricing, "We need to do a better job of telling guys we are available for them at a multitude of price points."

Too little, too late. In the face of new competition from adversaries including the Dollar Shave Club and Harry's, some reports show Gillette has relinquished market share for six straight years.

Gillette doubled down. Now believing that consumers are driven by price, they made this announcement: "You told us our blades can be too expensive, and we listened."

---

4 Procter & Gamble purchased Gillette in 2005 and reportedly allows it to direct its marketing. The Dollar Shave Club sold to Unilever for a billion dollars in 2016 and Harry's was reportedly bought by Edgewell Personal Care in 2019 for $1.37 billion.

They might as well have said, "You're right, our products are just like everybody else's, only we were a lot more expensive. Sorry about the decades of price-gouging. We will drop our prices."

Too bad, because with an emotion-based strategy, Gillette could achieve heartshare. Combined with their existing mindshare, they could weather this storm and get back to dominating their market.

And they wouldn't have to look far to find heartshare connections.

Founded by the entrepreneur King C. Gillette, the company issued razors for World War I soldiers who shaved each day, even in the trenches. With its distinctive history, Gillette has helped us look our best for everything from job interviews to first dates to weddings for over a century.

Perhaps Gillette could root through their journals and use their long history as emotional arsenal to take on these new competitors.

By emotionally connecting their audience with their products and not competing on price, Gillette could pull their audience back in—rather than push them away to compare products.

BUT—IF YOU AIM AT THE HEART, YOU BETTER HIT IT.

GILLETTE'S FOLLOW-UP CAMPAIGN attempted to redefine the brand's long-established slogan "the best a man can get" with a new theme, "Your best never comes easy."

This approach tried to align their brand with the real-life story of Shaquem Griffin's challenging journey to become the first one-handed linebacker in the NFL.

It's an emotionally moving campaign that shoots at the heart—but misses. By relying on something other than their own emotional currency, Gillette stands beside the emotion, not in it. They confuse emotional presentation with emotional connection and most importantly, they overvalue what people want to buy by undervaluing why they want to buy it.

In the 1947 book *The Five Great Rules of Selling,* author Percy Whiting quotes advertising executive Leo McGivena: *"Last year over one million quarter-inch drills were sold—not because people wanted quarter-inch drills but because they wanted quarter-inch holes."*

People don't buy a product; they buy the benefit it provides.

It's the valuable differentiator between using emotion in your presentation of a product and the presentation of an emotional connection with a product's benefits. It's something Gillette should consider because no one wants to buy a razor (even if it has five Fusion blades). But they do want to look better and feel good.

It's an easy assumption to believe people want better shaver efficiency, sharper edges, smoother glide strips and a longer blade life. But this only articulates **what** they want, not **why** they want it.

In 2019, Gillette took another step toward emotional persuasion with their wildly viral ad, a father teaching his trans son to shave. It's a brave ad presenting a compelling issue that Gillette aimed at the heart, not the head. To their credit, it got a lot of social media attention and was featured across a wide range of media outlets.

The Gillette ad team clearly expected the emotion in the ad to transfer to a relationship between viewers and Gillette razors. But it is a bridge too far. Emotion is generated, but it's connected to the story, not the product. Which is fine, unless you're trying to sell razors.

It's a subtle nuance. Emotional presentation versus emotional connection, and Gillette misses the opportunity.

Gillette tried, and I give them full credit. Further, because it's always easier to throw a rock than it is to build a window, I'd like to offer an example of how Gillette could have taken that extra step. In this imaginary ad, they emotionally connect their brand, their history and their products with their audience. (And sell some damn razors.)

OPENING SCENE: 1966 bathroom, small, intimate. Gillette shaving foam can on the shelf in front of the mirror.

The camera presents a close-up of a man's hand holding a single-blade safety razor. He swishes it in water and double-taps it on the ceramic sink, making a distinct sound.

The camera pans back to show a 35-year-old man puffing out his shaving foam-covered cheek as he drags the Gillette single blade razor across his face.

The camera pans wider until it includes a five-year-old, staring up, mesmerized at the man shaving. Off camera, the splashing and double-tap sound of the razor against the ceramic accompanies the scene.

The announcer's voice-over:
K. C. Gillette filed his patent for the first safety razor in 1901.

SCENE TWO: Same mid-'60s bathroom.

The man, now finished shaving, rubs his open hand and thumb over his clean-shaven cheek and jawline while smiling at his child.

SCENE THREE: Same bathroom, slightly updated to 1971 (shaving foam can is updated).

A close-up of the man's hand removing the blade before closing the safety razor and giving it to his son, who is now nine.

The camera pans back to show the boy standing on his toes, straining to see the reflection of his face covered in shaving cream as he pulls the bladeless razor over his cheek.

Behind him the man says, "With the grain, son," as he guides the boy's hand. The camera stays on the boy as he swishes the razor and double-taps the sink, replicating the exact sound and motion his father made in the first scene.

SCENE FOUR: Same 1971-style bathroom, scene extension.

The man checks his face in the mirror, rubbing his cheek and jawline as before while he glances down at his son. The camera pans back to include the boy, with a little dab of shaving foam still on one ear as he mimics his dad's hand motion on his own face.

SCENE FIVE: Same bathroom, late '70s, slightly updated decor and fashion.

The boy, now 16, holds a Gillette double razor. Half the shaving cream still on his face, he swishes the razor under the water and double-taps it. The camera pans back to include the bathroom doorway and the father (now 45) as he stops to peek in through the open bathroom doorway. The man doesn't say anything, just smiles at his son and drags his hand across his cheek and down his jawline before exiting the scene.

SCENE SIX: Scene extension.

The son, finished shaving, looks in the mirror and says with teenage sarcasm, "I know, Dad, with the grain." Then the scene cuts to the teen's reflection as he strokes his cheek and jawline and his expression changes to sudden surprise at the smoothness of his skin as the voice-over states…

Voice-over:

Later, Gillette added more blades for an even smoother shave.

SCENE SEVEN:

The son holds a baby on his lap as his father watches. The baby reaches up and rubs her daddy's face, smiling. The grandfather reaches up unconsciously and rubs his jaw as his son looks over and smiles.

SCENE EIGHT:

The original bathroom (unchanged since 1980).

The camera shows a close-up of an older man's hand shaving with the new Gillette razor. It is swished in water and double-tapped against the sink, then the razor makes another pass through the shaving cream in silence.

SCENE NINE: The original bathroom (scene extension).

The camera pans back to show two men. The boy, now 55, stands behind his seated father, now 85. He looks at his father in the mirror, smiles and reaches past him to swish the razor and double-tap it on the sink. He continues to shave his dad's cheek, saying calmly, "I know, Dad, with the grain."

SCENE TEN: Same bathroom, the final scene.

We see the two men in the bathroom mirror just after shaving. The father is seated, the son standing behind him. The camera pans in on the old man as he raises his shaking and fragile hand towards his face and strokes his cheek and jawline. He smiles in silence. The camera pans wider to show the son nodding slightly. He smiles back at his father and strokes his own cheek and jawline.

Voice-over:

Gillette—we have always been there to help you be your best.

Defining what a market segment wants is an important part of improving product features. But relying on these functions to sell a product (like *two scoops of raisins* and *three ounces of moisturizer*) leaves a company wide open to attacks from competitors with superior features or better pricing.

Features support the audience's default decisions, which, as we know, are temporary and available to the highest bidder or the lowest price. But emotional connection is a brand's fortress against the competition's attack.

Dunkin' Donuts coffee may cost less than Starbucks. But try and talk a Starbuckian out of their addiction to the little Green and White Crack Shack by explaining the comparative quality and price points.

Some companies understand the powerful difference between emotional connection and emotional presentation. Others miss this nuance and do their best to entice customers with what advertisers call "a bowl of onions," in their "make 'em cry to make 'em buy" approach. Many get the tears, yet few get the connection or the customers. Griffin's story moves people, but it doesn't move them to buy a razor from Gillette.

But what happens when mindshare is combined with the power of emotional connection and aimed at the audience's heart, not the head?

MINDSHARE + HEARTSHARE = MARKET SHARE

DURING A CHRISTMAS VISIT TO THE IN-LAWS, our motivation to stay indoors was intensified by thermometer readings that, when combined with the windchill, rivaled the temperatures on Mars. (I wish I was exaggerating.)

We experienced an old-fashioned Christmas, connecting over puzzles and board games and indulging in my favorite holiday pastime, watching the World Junior Hockey Championships.

The colder it got, the more hockey we watched. And the more advertising we consumed. Commercials, typically avoided with our PVR, were instead viewed in real time by a captivated audience.

Most came and went without notice, but one ad grabbed the entire room's attention and held us in mesmerized silence. It was a President's Choice message that connected their brand with our emotions.

The ad showed a collection of people in an assortment of life's greatest experiences while we listened to an audio recording of the late 20th-century British philosopher Alan Watts.

"So, let's suppose that you were able every night to dream any dream you wanted to dream. And that you could, for example, have the power within one night to dream 75 years of time. Or any length of time you wanted to have. And naturally, as you began on this adventure of dreams, you would fulfill all your wishes. You would have every kind of pleasure. And after several nights of 75 years of total pleasure each, you would say 'Woah, that was pretty great!' But now let's, um, let's have a surprise. Let's have a dream which isn't under my control. Well, something is gonna happen to me that I don't know what it's gonna be. And you did that, and came out of it and say 'Wow, that was a close shave, wasn't it?' Then you would get more and more adventurous and you would make further and further out gambles as to what you would dream and finally, you would dream where you are now ..."

The voice-over goes silent as the last scene shows the people we've seen throughout the film gathering around the dinner table, family and friends. The ad ends as the screen fills with the words, "Eat together. President's Choice."

It's a revolutionary approach. Rather than trying to connect with millions of individual memories, the ad entices viewers to access their own memories of joining a dinner table surrounded by the people they love. It evokes personal emotion and connects it with the President's Choice brand.

They could have relied on details to promote their brand, such as: "Studies have found couples who share three to four meals together every week are more likely to stay married; families who share meals have more college graduates in the household than families that don't eat together."

But they didn't. Instead, they used emotional connection. They chose magic over logic.

President's Choice connects by placing their emotional message close to the audience's heart. This ad motivates each person in a very diverse audience to recall their own memories and compassionately relate these experiences with the brand's message. If a picture is worth a thousand words, then the value of this approach is immeasurable. With it, President's Choice acquired heartshare, mindshare, market share—and of course—wallet share.

But not everyone believes in this revolutionary approach. Old habits, beliefs and values are often hard to break, and many can't abandon the delivery of logic, facts and features when they present.

» Maxwell House: *"Better Beans Make Better Coffee"* (Recently replaced with *"Good Just Got Better."*) (Sigh.)

» Verizon: *"Better Matters"*

» Smirnoff: *"Exclusively for Everybody"*

» Gillette: *"The Best a Man Can Get"* (1989 -2019)

These fact-and-feature-based brand messages leave the door wide open for new competitors.

Sorry, Kellogg's, I like your cereal, but I'd toss your flakes for a competitor with three scoops. Gillette, I have to admit, I'm now a Harry's razor man because the prices were better—and well, I just don't see the difference in the products.

EMOTIONAL PERSUASION — THE DARK ART

WHILE FACTS AND FEATURES ARE EASY TO SPOT, emotional persuasion isn't. Even though most people are aware of the advertiser's true intent, presenting to an audience's emotions without them being aware of it allows persuaders to connect unemotional objects (dog food, soap, SUVs, etc.) to the audience's most emotion-laden memories.

The process forms a bridge over skepticism, connecting the offer and the audience by triggering memories that establish an emotional connection, changing **what we think** about something into **how we feel** about it.

Persuaders know that transporting an audience beyond thinking and into feeling is the core of manipulation.

In his book *The Feeling of What Happens,* neuroscientist Antonio Damasio explains, "We are vulnerable when we are only vaguely aware that our emotions are being influenced, and most vulnerable when we have no idea at all that our emotions are being influenced."

While most marketers concentrate on how their audience thinks, the best know that what's more important is how their audience feels. They focus on influencing the shared nature of human emotions. This is important because thoughts are private, protected, individual and inaccessible—while emotions are general, common and vulnerable.

If you suffer from claustrophobia in small spaces, yet I experience coulrophobia and shudder at the sight of a clown, even though these are intensely personal anxieties, they share the same emotional common denominator: fear.

The common denominator is the key to influencing a diverse audience.

Whatever the personal experiences that created the memory (like a certain sixth birthday party featuring BOJO the Clown with his nicotine teeth and weapons-grade halitosis) they are deeply guarded, while the resulting emotional triggers are common and easily accessible.

I don't have to present clowns to one person and lock another in a tight space to evoke emotional responses. All I have to do is connect the audience with the relevant emotion (in this case, fear) and from there they will connect it back into their own experience. This is where the motivation to act resides.

If you want to buy a condominium as a home for your family, and someone else wants one as an investment, and a third person wants to buy a condo as their retirement home, each buyer has a different reason, related to their own needs. But if condo prices in the area begin to escalate and selection is disappearing, these buyers all share the same emotional motivation, fear of loss.

Plainly put, even though our experiences are unique, a persuader's effort to influence doesn't have to be specific to each individual, because human beings share a general set of emotions.

The palace never sleeps, but the palace guard does.

EMOTIONAL COMMONALITIES

ONE THEORY, WIDELY ACCEPTED among revolutionary psychologists, is that our emotions evolved to assist with survival and reproduction.

Species that experience emotions such as fear and anxiety have a heightened sense of awareness and response to danger, which aids survival and, ultimately, procreation.

We stay aware to stay alive.

This makes emotion **universally consistent**, rather than specific to each social or cultural environment. However, differences do exist. Not with emotion itself, but with the way each culture **reacts** to certain emotions.

Although this is an oversimplification of persuasion's effect on culturally influenced reactions, there are three main differentiators to think about when predicting which approach will be most effective.

In the West, our individualist culture values independence. A person's uniqueness is important. People are encouraged to outwardly express their inner emotions and react according to the emotional expression of others. The expressive display of emotional reaction is encouraged.

In the individualist cultures, it is generally acceptable to use emotions to influence others, such as smiling and saying, "Have a great day" or being overly excited to influence an audience with enthusiasm. It's not just Tony Robbins' content that entices his audience—his emotional charisma is contagious.

Western cultures are more inclined to participate in activities that produce a high level of emotional stimuli, such as sports with a higher degree of contact like football, lacrosse and hockey.

It is typical for parents in this culture to encourage their children's involvement in these activities, as well as to promote the outward expression of emotion. Marketing to the western individualist culture is successful when it considers this social transference of enthusiasm. Using language that generates emotional reward for individualistic behavior, like describing achieved wealth as "financial independence" and getting "ahead of the crowd," is like a dog whistle that silently triggers behavior.

Focusing on the individual versus the group is at the core of this approach. (Charitable organizations achieve stronger results by presenting individuals that need help rather than an entire group of people in need.)

Marketing to this culture is successful when the individual is presented as separate and positioned as standing out from the group. ("Are you a man or a sheep?") This vernacular often rewards independent action by positioning the "general public" as the adversary of the liberated thinker.

By rewarding singularity, this approach often incorporates **inclusion** of the individual through the **exclusion** of another group. *"Subscribe and receive insider access unavailable to the general public."*

When presenting to collectivist (generally Eastern) cultures, on the other hand, the emphasis should be on personal achievement that doesn't come at the expense of others.

This culture values interdependency and places high importance on fitting in rather than standing out. It reacts favorably to group reward and low emotional stimulation. Controlling emotional reactions, rewarding those who conform and discouraging outward displays of emotion to influence others are emphasized.

For effective marketing and communication when attempting to influence collectivist cultures, presentations geared toward group emotions, collaboration and achieving harmony over independence are the most persuasive.

Messages must focus on self-discipline, harmony and loyalty and emphasize family and work relationships. Honor is above all.

Emotional persuasion that shows the achievement of a common objective above individual needs will generate the strongest reaction. Because of the focus on harmony within the group, collectivist cultures can have a strong fear of rejection. Unlike the individualistic culture's fear of **missing out**, for the interdependence culture it is fear of being **left out** that has the strongest impact.

The third culture is a hybrid that praises materialistic motivation and survival values (economic prominence, monetary and personal security). They exist within the interdependent culture and appreciate low emotional stimulation but react to emotional persuasion that offers improved cultural ranking. Prizing survival values that relate to self-importance, this group responds emotionally to marketing offering a reward for action that is connected to high visibility and individual importance within the group.

Being perceived by their peers as financially successful is as important as being financially successful. One local campaign that spoke directly to this group positioned an artist's rendering of a new high-rise tower as a reflection in the windshield of a new luxury vehicle accompanied with the headline "*Be Seen.*"

Each culture experiences emotional stimuli the same way internally, but reacts differently externally.

Sigmund Freud believed that as we grow up in a society, we internalize its social virtues; this leads to the development of our personalities.

While Freud was accurate in his assessment, it is interesting to consider that at the time of his theory, change was happening at a much slower pace.

Now, with rapidly changing social stimuli, each generation experiences multiple new influences as they mature. Easier access to international communication, travel and information has influenced the generation known as Millennials. As a result, they tend not to collect objects like previous generations; instead, they collect emotional experiences. For them, a collection of passport stamps is even better than an expensive running shoe collection.

In other words, today's persuaders must understand the rapidly changing values of their audience and how different cultures and generations respond to emotionally persuasive marketing.

A few years ago, I was hired as a consultant to launch a double high-rise tower for a developer in Montreal. At the time, their typical local buyer profile had grown up renting and focused on attaining lifestyle; home ownership had little emotional appeal.

I shifted the campaign, marketing more broadly and toward a different culture, people who did value home ownership. This enabled us to reach more potential buyers who were emotionally motivated to achieve home ownership. The result was a level of success not before seen in the history of projects marketed and sold in that city's downtown core.

But it wasn't a wider reach that drove success—it was being aware of the cultural shifts at work and targeting emotional persuasion toward the appropriate audience.

CHAPTER 14

WHO NEEDS TO PERSUADE? WE ALL DO.

UNDERSTANDING THE ART OF EMOTIONAL INFLUENCE enables you to survive and succeed. Whether it's a date, a new job or an investor you're looking for, your future depends on your ability to persuade. And your financial future depends on being able to protect your emotions and wallet from those who want access.

From drill presses to lawn mowers to body wash, most things we purchase are unemotional objects. (With the exception of coffee—it's always there for me, it understands me, it just loves me back.) So why is it common for consumers to have an emotional attachment to a certain brand or their products?

The trick up every effective persuader's sleeve is to focus on emotionally connecting the audience with the experience the product provides.

The best persuaders know that products, unable to produce an emotional connection based on their function, must focus on the *emotional benefits* they provide. (Just ask a John Deere owner how they feel about their green tractors and ride-a-mowers. Feel, not think.)

But finding a product's emotional benefit and connecting it to the audience isn't easy. As we've discussed, even large corporations with enormous budgets give up and resort to presenting facts and features.

An illustration of this is Esso's recent advertising approach. The company spends millions in marketing, but their campaigns often abandon emotion completely.

In a recent effort, perhaps Esso believed the audience would be as enamored with gasoline as they are. (Or they simply couldn't find an emotional connection.)

The advertising focused on the perfection of their gasoline's ingredients and promoted product superiority, ingredient supremacy and the company's attention to detail—rather than the emotional benefits and solutions their product provides.

Esso's ads feature an articulate, spectacle-wearing scientist who explains, *"We are ridiculous about being meticulous, right down to the seven meticulously balanced ingredients in Synergy gasoline. Meticulously designed to help protect your engine and improve fuel economy. Maybe it's because we are obsessive.*

Or maybe it's because we care."

Someone watching this ad could be drawn in by the idea of being "ridiculous about being meticulous." After all, our families depend on gasoline reliability every time we get in a car. But then Esso's marketing takes a wrong turn with statements like, "designed to help protect your engine and improve fuel economy." Come on!

If Esso was as meticulous about influencing their potential customers as they were about protecting our engines, they could have pulled away from their gasoline's features and driven towards emotionally connecting us with how their product is critically beneficial to our well-being.

No, emotional connection isn't easy. But, as with most products that don't transfer well emotionally, the technique is to focus on the emotional value of the benefits they provide. So, it is a matter of presenting not how the gasoline functions in our cars, but how its benefits help us function in our lives.

No one wants to buy gas, but everyone wants to get somewhere.

Esso might have considered how we drive our kids to hockey practice and dance recitals, travel on our summer vacations, plant crops and deliver food—all of this using and relying on their product. We provide, produce, accomplish and nurture because of gasoline. This makes the number of potential emotional connections between Esso's product and their audience virtually endless.

Esso, your product doesn't protect my engine, it protects my family.

Esso did attempt emotional connection in their European campaign, "Journeys That Matter." They produced a series of mini-videos presenting people on different journeys, but they forced the emotion of the actors onto the audience. Rather than allowing the audience to connect through their own experience, Esso positioned themselves as the authority on how we should feel.

In one journey, an elderly lady is determined to visit an old flame. After driving for what seems like months through rain and snow, even sleeping in her car, she eventually reaches her destination, unannounced, to meet her long-lost love.

The entire campaign was an attempt at emotional connection. But it presented an unemotional reenactment of an actor's memories. We might be touched by the elderly lady's tenacity and moved by her courage. But few people have slept in their car in order to visit an old flame; in fact, most of us can't think of a worse idea. So, while we may appreciate her eventual success at reconnecting, the campaign's content and message fail to evoke personal emotions. We don't see ourselves in her journey, so we can't relate or empathize. We definitely don't connect.

Again, there is only a subtle difference between emotional connection and emotional presentation. If that connection is missed, while it may entertain, it doesn't influence.

The presentation of an emotional experience should arouse the emotions the audience has felt on their own journeys. It should then connect the benefits of its product with the emotions our mind has connected with those experiences. It's at that point we are most easily influenced.

Esso's campaign was an expensive attempt that failed to push the audience beyond their default position that all gas is the same—so why not choose the gas station that is closest or cheapest right now?

By understanding what is emotionally relevant to their audience, persuaders can align their product benefits (not functions or features) with their audience's personal experiences. This evokes emotional connectivity, reduces cognitive processing and ultimately increases the product's value.

That's exactly how a little Korean car company took a big chunk out of their competition.

Up against some well-established brands, Kia was the underdog of the automotive industry. But they had a secret weapon. When Kia introduced their compact model, the Kia Soul, into the crowded low-price vehicle sector, they did it by getting emotionally relevant.

They connected the Kia Soul with the Gen Y and Millennial car-buying audience and their lifestyle influences in music, technology, fashion and pop culture. Kia aligned the Soul with the audience's self-image of who they believed they were—and most importantly, evoked emotion by identifying who, and what, they were not. Kia connected beyond thinking, by prompting feelings.

The car company leaned on their agency David&Goliath to create television ads that featured human-sized hamsters bouncing to hip-hop inside a vibrant fire-engine-red Kia Soul.

The ad's imagery, purposefully rebellious, was an emotional synonym that presented the Soul weaving through other wide-eyed, envious rodents running in place on their hamster wheels—wheels of dreary conformity.

The campaign connected and Kia's sales jumped 36 percent in 2009 compared to the industry's 10-percent average, outselling powerhouses Toyota and Ford by a wide margin in the category. Along the way, Kia won Automotive Ad of the Year and a prestigious Effie award for advertising effectiveness.

Kia's follow-up campaign presented their hooded hamsters in the new Soul as the hip-hop song "The Choice is Yours" pounded out the lyrics, "you can get with this, or you can get with that ...." While the ad's imagery connected the "*This*" with the unique Kia Soul, and the "*That*" with boring toasters and washing machine metaphors, representing Kia's unimaginative competitors.

The hamster commercials generated more than 20 million online views. Kia's sales exploded from 32,000 units in 2009 to over 115,000 three years later, spurring multiple years of double-digit growth in the U.S. and solidifying the brand's appeal.

By the end of this book, you'll have the tools you need to replicate Kia's success—and to resist the siren song of Kia's adorable and persuasive hamsters.

A BRAND'S EMOTIONAL PROMISES

A BRAND WITHOUT AN EMOTIONAL PROMISE is just a company with a product.

Kia, Coke, Apple and Nike are examples of brands that communicate an emotional promise to connect well beyond the products they sell.

We know Nike doesn't sell computers and Apple doesn't sell shoes—although, if Apple decided to sell runners, we'd expect them to be stylish, sleek, technologically advanced and incredibly well designed. We would expect the shoes to be all of these things because of Apple's commitment to their brand's emotional promise.

Nike does sell shoes, among other things, all based on an emotional brand promise that has little to do with pitching athletic wear.

Their grey and white ads feature sweat-covered, intensely competitive star athletes, but the ads aren't about shoes or shirts. They present Nike's brand promise, to help us with our own potential to be great.

Coke's product is a carbonated sugary drink. It's recognized and consumed around the world, yet Coke's marketing has little to do with the product, and everything to do with emotion. "Have a Coke and a smile" is their core message. The brand's eternally emotional promise is to provide an experience, a feeling that makes any moment special.

Emotional branding is the promise to deliver a reward—the product, service or offering—at a dimension equal to or exceeding the customer's expectation of value. This is something that goes far beyond the functionality of the product.

A brand's emotional promise impacts the level of desire for a product. And because emotion dictates the value audiences place on a product, it ultimately influences what they are willing to pay.

> We know that emotion dictates human decisions, action and values, while detail evokes the human need to compare. So why would anyone, ever, market anything using details rather than emotion?

Consider how time is kept by a Patek Philippe watch compared to a Timex. Different products. Similar, if not identical, functionality. Yet the audience's anticipation of reward is based not on function, but on each brand's emotional promise—and this makes the consumer's perception of value very different.

My first watch, a Timex, was a gift from my parents. Back then the Timex brand promise of durability and reliability was presented in their ads and slogan: "Timex. It takes a licking and keeps on ticking."

Their campaigns featured the "Timex Torture Test." Strapped to the bow of a speedboat, taped to a homerun hitter's baseball bat or tossed in a washing machine, the watch took a beating. And each time it emerged unaffected, still keeping perfect time.

On the other hand (or wrist), I found a gold Patek Philippe Grand with an alligator band for $367,410 online (but shipping was free). And while the functions are similar, you probably won't find a Patek Philippe strapped to the bow of a boat.

The Patek Philippe brand promise strives to achieve a specific value by connecting their watch with the highest quality and elite luxury, and something far removed from time—emotional gratification.

For more than 20 years, their campaigns have featured fathers with their sons and the slogan, "You never actually own a Patek Philippe. You merely look after it for the next generation." It isn't about keeping correct time or about time at all. It's about investing in a generational purchase that promises the pride of passing on an heirloom.

I'm sure Mom and Dad had this in mind as I unwrapped my Timex.

Different brand promises, delivering very different paths to value. One functional—the other, emotional. The difference between emotion and function? About $367,371.

Emotional branding is the commitment to deliver something that increases the audience's anticipation of emotional reward and their perception of its value. And, just like beauty, value is in the eye of the beholder.

The best persuaders know their audience's perceived value is related to something greater than simply fulfilling a need. The bigger the impact on the audience's feelings, the stronger their desire for ownership, and the greater the influence it will have on their life.

The role of an emotional brand promise is to inspire the audience's expectations by creating a perception of value that is greater than the product's individual components and functions.

Some understand this power and present their brand as an emotional promise that improves their audience's life.

Early on, Coke stopped selling a sugary drink that was created to cure hangovers, anxiety and low libidos, and started selling emotion. Coke transformed their brand from a **beverage into a feeling**. (In an ironic twist, this was about the same time cocaine was removed from the recipe.)

Volvo's brand promise is strength and safety. Even their logo is shaped like an ancient chemical sign for iron. And while their campaigns focus on safety, the car company presents product functionality as an emotional benefit—*if you care about the well-being of your family, you'll buy a Volvo.*

Brands that connect with their audience's emotions succeed in achieving heartshare; they increase the audience's perception of their value.

One brand taking the opposite approach, focusing on functionality, is Hyundai. They first entered the market competing in the lower-end price range with a quality-challenged product. Years ago, a friend purchased one of the first Hyundai cars in our area. I remember popping open the sunroof only to watch the glass shoot up like an ejector seat and land on the road behind us in thousands of pieces. Years later, Hyundai still struggles to overcome this original impression, even though their quality has substantially improved. But rather than using emotional connection to resolve this gap between its products and its market, the company goes all in on function.

Hyundai dismissed the heart, confronting their audience's perception of reliability by offering a 10-year, 100,000-mile warranty. Kudos for delivering what is among the longest guarantees in the car industry—but without emotion, their brand's perceived value remains unchanged, only better protected. Now their audience's perception is connected to the warranty, not to the Hyundai brand. Once the warranty is removed, their perceived value will, like my friend's sunroof, be shattered. Short-term gain, but long-term pain.

Enhancing your audience's value perception should be at the core of your emotional promise. It is a commitment to improving the emotional aspects of your customer's life, like associating a beverage with a feeling of joy or the pride experienced in the legacy of an heirloom watch. A brand promising to remove the risk of owning their product just doesn't deliver a positive emotional experience, as much as we might love a 10-year warranty.

Get the emotional brand promise right and the effects on value are incredible. Get it wrong, and the results may be disastrous.

GETTING IT RIGHT, THEN GETTING IT WRONG— THE STORY OF CANADA'S LITTLE BANK THAT COULD, THEN COULDN'T.

IN AN EFFORT TO EXPAND, Canada's third-largest lender, the Bank of Nova Scotia, acquired ING Bank of Canada and rebranded it in 2014 as Tangerine Bank.

While most Canadian banks competed by adding features like longer hours, increased convenience and hassle-free Internet banking, Tangerine's approach was different.

Tangerine skipped the features and hit the emotions. They got it right and connected emotionally with the largely underserviced target audience of middle-class working Canadians.

Tangerine aligned their brand with the audience's self-image by advertising images of working folks tenaciously striving in their challenging work conditions. The ads connected the audience's belief in their own work ethic with Tangerine's emotional brand-promise, *"wanting hardworking folks to keep more of their hard-earned money."*

The campaign resonated with their audience and Tangerine reported a staggering 295 percent increase in new clients.

They got it right—but then, they got it wrong.

After reaching the pinnacle, Tangerine exchanged emotional connection for product evangelization.

Tangerine's initial emotional advertising attracted attention and initiated action; but their follow-up ads focused on features. As a result, Tangerine lost its hard-won heartshare. Worse, the presentation of their product details motivated customers to think about, of all things, checking out the competition.

> The art of persuasion is the ability to identify an audience's beliefs about who they are, present your offering as relevant to this belief, and emotionally connect it with benefits that will improve the way they feel about their lives.

THE EMOTION OF PRICE

FACTS AND FEATURES FAIL TO PROVIDE ACCESS to your audience's emotions. Yet one fact that does have an emotional connection is price.

Price is persuasive because it's related to value. Yet many presenters misunderstand this relationship, and too often price is the victim in misguided efforts to influence. If presented correctly, with supporting components, price has a strong impact. If used incorrectly, it can have a negative effect.

The challenge is that price is based on the audience's **perception** of comparative value, as with a Timex versus a Patek Philippe watch. This makes value subject to variables such as preference, need and other factors.

This means that price, while a fact, is experienced irrationally. Consider a price reduction. While some may see the new price as an opportunity, others may see it as a reflection of lower quality.

Because we aren't hardwired with independent assessment meters, we use comparison to achieve our perception of value in the absence of emotion.

Take shopping for a new car as an example. Perhaps fuel efficiency is important to you—but this detail has no value unless it can be compared against the fuel efficiency of other cars.

Car lots post the "Manufacturer's Suggested Retail Price" on each new car's window—without it, how would we know if the dealer's price is good?

By supporting price with elements such as environment (think of a Tiffany's store) or controlled comparables, such as a manufacturer's suggested retail price, persuaders can influence our assessment meter and take our instinct to compare offline.

In this way, price can move beyond being a fact and take on emotion to ultimately influence value.

THE PRICE OF PIE

WHEN I WAS SIX, my family moved to the sleepy seaside town of White Rock and my father bought a little bakery that sat across the road from the beach. I guess you could say it was an impulse purchase, because even though Dad had been a baker early in his life, he hadn't made a loaf of bread in years. But since we'd just left a winter storm in the Canadian Prairies to land in West Coast sunshine, that little bakery overlooking the beach and ocean waves was too tempting to pass up.

Over the years, the business grew, and customers filled the little shop. Each day at closing, everything was sold. Everything except for the pies.

Dad just couldn't sell his pies. "A bakery," he said, "must sell pies." He tried different recipes, new varieties, made them larger, smaller, fancier. Nothing worked.

Dinner conversations were always filled with bakery talk, and usually we ended up on the topic of why the pies weren't selling.

After trying everything, Dad happened to be chatting with the owner of a huge retail store and explained how the summers brought in hordes of tourists but even with slashed pricing, it was rare to sell a pie.

"Triple the price," the fellow suggested. Dad thanked him politely for his comments and left the store.

The summer rush arrived as the hot weather returned and the little bakery again felt like it would burst at the seams. But still no pies were sold.

With zero to lose, Dad pulled out the felt marker, tripled the pie prices and retreated into the back to ready himself for a customer revolt.

After the last customer left and the front staff locked the doors, Dad pulled off his white apron and ventured out. Head down, he approached the pie rack, mentally preparing to accept this latest pie failure.

Every pie was gone.

It was price that sold the pies, just not in the way Dad expected. His quality-conscious customers self-influenced their value perception of his pies based on everything else in the environment.

"If a product in this bakery is expensive, it must be worth it."

We never ate leftover pie again. But even to this day, I still say no to dessert.

Value is based on perception, and perception is emotionally influenced. In the right environment, a higher price can intensify perception of value. It's something luxury brands have been leveraging since the dawn of consumerism.

In Robert Cialdini's book *Influence, the Psychology of Persuasion*, he describes a similar story about a friend who can't sell her turquoise jewelry. In Cialdini's story, the shop owner instructs her saleslady to price the entire lot at half off. The confused clerk prices the collection at double the price. Of course it all sells.

Cialdini explains that this phenomenon is based upon triggered instincts that are related to our "fixed-action patterns" and "standard principles of stereotyping." In other words, jewelry customers equate expensive with good.

What I love about Cialdini's description is his explanation of the human need to classify things (stereotype, as he puts it) for the sake of efficiency.

In his book, one of the most dramatic statements is that, due to our existence in "an extraordinarily complicated stimulus environment," we need to process complex situations. To do this, we need shortcuts.

He explains that we "classify things according to a few key features and then respond mindlessly when one of these trigger features is present."

As discussed earlier, I experienced this at a very young age in our family's bakery.

Our world is a complicated place and we've developed processes to analyze and manage everything we encounter.

These processes have been updated over millennia so that each new experience, environment or incoming stimulus doesn't need explicit, time-consuming dissection. We see a new situation, recognize similarities from past experience and add it to our repertoire for quick access and retrieval next time.

I will add to Cialdini's observations: Because our behavior is impacted by our surroundings, the environments we enter have a dramatic influence on our emotions. This means the environment itself is an active persuader. And once triggered by an environment, our emotions overpower our logic to control our decisions and actions. Design your environment to relay the right emotions—and you will influence those within it.

CHAPTER 15

WHY EMOTIONAL ENVIRONMENTS IMPACT VALUE *(THE SECRET RECIPE FOR MOTIVATING CROWDS)*

"Don't talk, don't run, and for god's sake, <u>don't</u> touch anything."
— Field trip supervisors everywhere —

WE'D BEEN ON SCHOOL FIELD TRIPS BEFORE, but this time, like the rest of the kids on that bus, I was more excited about the long journey than our museum destination.

Museums, after all, were boring, packed with glass-enclosed objects guarded by uniformed security watching our every move. For a 12-year-old, there wasn't a less fun place on the planet. But after driving for hours, the novelty of travel, like the bus seat's padding, had worn thin. Anything, even a museum, would be better. Finally we arrived, the bus parked, and we sprinted for the entrance.

THE ROYAL BC MUSEUM

THE FIREBALL ENERGY OF FIVE DOZEN PRETEENS poured through the museum's front doors, only to halt, mouths gaping, eyes wide.

We were greeted by soaring ceilings, towering totem poles and wide-open spaces. Everything on display was fully exposed, accessible, touchable—so different from the usual "don't touch anything" museums, it dared us to interact with this microcosm of an extraordinary planet.

Here, I wasn't an outsider peering through glass at untouchable artifacts from Captain Cook's voyage—I was inside his ship.

My hands felt the frayed ropes and weathered sailcloth; the air was thick with the smell of old wood, tar and the sea. Gulls cried overhead while the ship's hull creaked and rubbed against its moorings.

I practically ran from one exhibit to the next as if traversing time. Leaving a 20th-century working gold mine, I stepped into the Ice Age, a barren landscape dominated by a life-sized woolly mammoth. I journeyed back to the turn of the century and walked on cobblestone streets, wandered through a 150-year-old hotel and sat in a silent movie theater watching Charlie Chaplin. Every sense was activated; the environment took complete emotional control.

Back home, I dominated the dinner table with stories of my great adventure and begged my parents to bring us back to this magical place. It was the first time I'd been affected by an environment's emotional influence. It's something I wouldn't forget and a lesson I've relied upon when designing my own presentation centers, transforming them into emotion-generating environments.

If you have control of your presentation environment, it can be your most powerful persuasion tool. Environments are most effective when they emotionally present to both the conscious and the subconscious mind. It is much more than visual. Environments influence beyond thought; they influence feelings, where our decisions are made.

From retail shops to markets to museums, when the correct sensory combinations are achieved, an environment becomes emotionally persuasive, with the power to dictate the value of its offerings and the actions of the people who visit.

EMOTIONAL EXPERIENTIAL ENVIRONMENTS

BECAUSE WE REACT TO STIMULI ON MULTIPLE LEVELS, internal (interoceptive) and external (exteroceptive), our environment perception is simultaneously telescopic and microscopic. Without our knowledge, this multilevel interaction with our environment has a dramatic influence on the way we act within it. We are constantly accumulating and processing not only obvious information, but also the diminutive details.

From the fish tank in your dentist's office that calms pre-needle anxieties to the pace-decelerating music that keeps us shopping in the grocery aisles, each environmental element has the ability to generate the power of influence.

From breathing to sexual attraction, much of our life is dictated by the unconscious.

RESEARCH SHOWS THAT OUR UNCONSCIOUS is receiving and processing millions of bits of sensory information through our nervous system every second. So it's not just the visual imagery we absorb consciously, it's the environment's low-level stimuli, the things we take in subconsciously, that influence our behavior.

This is something professional persuaders understand. The use of subtle "low attention cues," as they're known, is called priming. This works similarly to product placement in movies and television, where products are placed in subtle locations to influence the audience's subconscious.

Priming an environment with low-attention communication amplifies the sensory representation of your offering; it influences thought processing and behavioral patterns.

An important subconscious communicator is an environment's tactile messages, like the table of cashmere sweaters at the front of the clothing store. The higher the hourly rate, the more luxurious the reception furnishings will be in your lawyer's office. Persuaders understand that strategically positioned tactile communicators connect at a deep sensory level (and prepare you for outrageous legal fees).

Similar to my museum experience, when an environment communicates on multiple levels, it connects emotionally. And that influences behavior.

I often wonder why most hotel registration desks are designed to be visually appealing rather than using their surfaces to deliver a tactile sensory representation of the business. If you have control over your own space and are not using it to communicate emotionally, you're missing an opportunity to connect and influence your audience.

HOT AND COLD RUNNING EMOTIONS

IN MY SALES AND PRESENTATION CENTERS, we serve hot drinks in handle-less mugs that transfer warmth to the recipient's hands. The display suites feature tactile experience-enhancing furniture and elements that beg to be touched. Outside the front entrances, there is calming music playing. Inside, aroma, sound and light subconsciously communicate the connecting message.

The best retailers set up power isles and path their visitors through tactile experiences. They understand subconscious communication and use it to influence behavior and generate a stronger customer connection.

In the competitive world of retail, it isn't a stretch to imagine a future where patrons wander the aisles while pushing buggies or carrying baskets that have low-attention communicators installed in their handles.

This isn't just anecdotal. Neurological research shows how subconsciously relayed messaging, such as touch, temperature and taste, impact emotion, influence human behavior and drive our decision processes.

In a study recently described in a *Harvard Business Review* article, people were asked to hold and evaluate either a warm or cold therapeutic pad. The researchers were testing how the participant's "thermoception sensation" would alter their behavior.

The experiment found that people invested 43 percent more money after briefly holding the warm pad compared to holding a cold pad. This suggests the physical sensation of warmth led people to feel psychologically warmer, safer and more trusting.

In other words, people subconsciously associated *tactile warmth* with the emotions of *comfort and security.* This influenced their behavior and they acted in a more purchase-positive way. It's something worth considering next time you're seated in a waiting room. Perhaps that leather sofa and hot coffee are actually an attempt to communicate.

While it may be challenging to introduce warmth into the hands of your own audience, it's prudent to take every opportunity and subconsciously convey trust, quality, warmth and respect in any way you can.

Every aspect of the environment plays a part in communicating your intended message. Temperature, imagery, sound, taste, smell, texture and proximity to others—it all matters. Think about the restaurants you've gone to with tables placed too close together, chairs too far apart, or lighting that's either too bright or too dim. Everything has a part to play in emotionally influencing your audience and connecting them with your offering.

Emotional response, a byproduct of the physical experience in a controlled environment, is incredibly influential in our perception of value.

Consider the purchase of a luxury vehicle. The perception of value is heavily influenced by environment. Imagine sitting in a new Mercedes with an interior featuring plastic fittings and cloth seats—how would the physical sensations influence your perception of its value?

Every physical environment is communicating something emotionally. The key is to maximize every opportunity to correspond beyond conscious awareness and interact with your audience's every sense.

IN ANOTHER STUDY featured in *the Harvard Business Review,* researchers considered the influence of tactile sensations.

In a series of tests, the participants (again, unaware of the researchers' true intentions) who sat on hard chairs negotiated harder than those who sat in soft chairs.

The results are worth paying attention to, as those in comfy, cushioned chairs offered an average of 28 percent more during negotiations than those sitting on rigid, uncomfortable chairs.

The article also mentioned a food retailer who increased sales by presenting an organic, earthy environment and using taste stations to give shoppers an opportunity to experience its products.

I know what you're thinking: Food sampling isn't new. But these taste stations were not designed to sell specific products. Instead, they communicated sensory connections to the environment.

In 2014, the *Journal of Consumer Psychology* published a special issue on embodiment and sensory perception, exploring how sensory inputs influenced consumer behavior. The researchers described non-conscious communication as **subconscious stimuli,** experienced by consumers who don't perceive it as marketing messages.

Because the stimuli are not perceived as marketing initiatives, they don't trigger typical consumer resistance.

When unconscious stimuli support conscious communication, your audience hears, sees, and, most importantly, feels what you are presenting.

The influence of subconscious and conscious connection dictates behavior—something I experienced firsthand on a golf cart.

WHOLE IN ONE

THE ANNUAL GOLF TOURNAMENT STARTED AS USUAL, player registration followed by obligatory tequila sampling.

Carts assigned, bags secured and coolers filled, we headed out on what promised to be a day packed full of laughter, free of seriousness or competition.

I look forward to this tournament all year. It's a great chance to catch up with old friends, laugh a lot, golf where scores don't matter and raise money for charity.

After lunch, we headed to the famous seventh fairway. It's a picturesque par three, only accessible through a long tunnel that travels under the highway. What makes it special is the sandy beach that surrounds the green as it juts off the coastline on a small peninsula.

This par three has a nasty reputation for being the most challenging in the area. It's not the fairway distance but the surging wind gusting off the ocean that makes it close to impossible to land a ball on the green.

Sandwiches finished, we hopped into our carts and drove down the path towards the tunnel. But this year we were in for a surprise; the long dark passageway had been lined with speakers pounding out the recorded sounds of speeding Formula One race cars.

Enveloped by the sounds of race car engines reverberating off the concrete walls, even our slow-moving golf carts felt like they were reaching breakneck speeds in the shadowy tunnel. We laughed out loud and raced the other carts towards the light. Outside, our eyes readjusted to the sunshine. Suddenly all laughter stopped.

There, surrounding the tee-off box, were five brand new Maserati Gran Turismos.

Hole-in-one prizes.

Lots of golf tournaments offer cars as prizes, but this was different. The combination of sound, touch, motion and visual stimuli connected with everyone on a sensory level.

Never have so many moderately inebriated golfers sobered up so quickly.

Jokes stopped. Seriousness took over. Conscious and subconscious receptors had been activated and our anticipation of emotional reward was amplified.

All you had to do was hit the ball 210 yards and sink it into a little cup about 2.5 times its size that resided at the base of a flag, which just happened to be snapping back and forth in 50-mile-per-hour gusts off the Pacific.

That day I didn't go home with a Gran Turismos (the Maseratis were in no danger of going anywhere but back to the dealership). But I did leave with an exceptional lesson in how combined stimuli can consciously and subconsciously communicate on a sensory level to influence action, intensify value and amplify the anticipation of a reward.

Fun Fact: The 2014 M5 BMW was designed to relay the engine's sound through its speakers—even when the stereo is turned off.

ENVIRONMENTS THAT SELL

DESIGNING A SALES OR PRESENTATION ENVIRONMENT? Start by asking what emotion you want it to communicate. This is critical when influencing anticipation of your product, service or offering's value. Without it, your environment may underperform. Subconsciously, your audience could then believe that your offering will follow suit.

Nike and Apple are two companies that understand how subconscious sensory components can combine to create emotional environments that support their brand's promise.

As mentioned earlier, Nike's brand objective is to elevate every athlete's potential, even those using their Bowflex Trainer as a sweater holder. This is reflected in Nike's retail environments. The company's SoHo store unites their emotional brand promise of improved personal performance with their retail environment to give shoppers a full emotional experience.

From their basketball half court to running coaches who analyze your performance while you sweat it out on their treadmills in front of wall-sized video screens, Nike's emotion-generating environments deliver their brand's promise on a sensory level.

Apple's retail model, "a place to improve, to learn, to be supported," shares Nike's aim to blend physical and emotional elements that merge their environment with their brand. Apple's objective is to elevate the visitor experience from **cerebral** to **emotional**, ultimately intensifying their customers' perception of value.

Retailers have the distinct advantage of environmental influence, yet many focus on optics and functionality, disregarding the power of subconscious communication.

A big part of the environment isn't what you sell in it, it's how you sell it.

"Wait here," he said, sliding past me to lock the front door. Pausing for a moment, glancing up and down the street, as if to make sure no one was watching, he then motioned for me to follow him with the slightest nod of his head. Past the shelves of cigars and boxes enclosed in glass cases, we headed through the long narrow shop. At the back we stopped. Once again, the storeowner looked cautiously towards the front door. I turned to look too, although I had no idea what I was looking for.

The small shop sold every kind of cigar and cigar accessory you could imagine, from elaborate cutters to humidors, and, of course, cigars from around the world.

Walking in was like stepping back in time. The hundred-year-old bank building still retained its rich architecture, even though its plaster walls now held the smell of tobacco leaves and cedar. The wooden floors creaked and complained, only adding to the ambience. But this paled in comparison to the experience awaiting anyone who asked for a Cuban cigar.

In Canada, there is nothing illegal about buying Cubans. As a matter of fact, they are stocked in most cigar stores. But in this little shop, telling the owner you wanted to buy a Cuban cigar was the beginning of an unforgettable experience.

Swinging open the old bank vault door, he motioned me inside the converted humidor. Cases of cigars piled on crates and boxes that were stacked to the ceiling. The choice was overwhelming.

With the shop locked and the vault door closing in just the two of us, I have to admit, I felt a little uneasy when he leaned in and asked, "Why Cuban?"

I hesitated, so he continued in a whispered tone, "Why do you want a Cuban cigar?" Leaning closer, he asked, "Is this a simple pleasure, a daily indulgence, or perhaps a special event?"

I found my footing and explained that I was going to see friends to celebrate the birth of our first son.

"A SON!" he boomed. "A baby boy! Then you must have Cohibas."

Grabbing a new wooden box and pulling a knife from his pocket, he sliced through the container's Republica De Cuba State seal. Unlatching the small brass clasp, he opened the lid and held the box for me to inspect.

Seeing I had no idea what I was looking for, he explained how the colors were a golden rich brown, each cap was perfect, the letters on the cigar band were embossed and the cigar's feel was perfect.

This wasn't a purchase; this was an education, an experience.

Over the next few years, I returned to the little shop to buy cigars and chat with Carlos, the owner, as he passionately discussed the history of Cuban culture and cigars.

When my second son was born, I realized I hadn't bought cigars in almost a year. I had a small pang of excitement as I parked and walked towards the shop. I wondered what Carlos would say about the birth of our second child.

I opened the door and stepped inside. A man who was not Carlos looked up from his chair.

"Where is Carlos?" I asked.

"He's gone. Sold. You want cigar?"

"Uh, I need Cohibas," I finally managed to say.

He simply pointed and said, "Back there."

I picked out a box and asked why the tobacco colors didn't match. The new owner just shrugged and asked how many I wanted. Like Carlos, the mystique was gone, and the unique experience along with it.

That was 14 years ago. It's a wedding dress shop now. Perhaps the new owner has figured out how to create an emotional environment (or at least get the smell of tobacco out of the dresses). I've wondered how

Carlos would do in today's online retail world. But I know it wouldn't be a problem because he understood emotional influence. He knew how to use his environment and everything in it to deliver an extraordinarily emotional experience.

AS CONSUMERS MINIMALIZE PRODUCT DIFFERENTIATION, their default decision hierarchy elevates the value of convenience. This pushes more people to save time by moving from bricks to clicks. Having something that you ordered in the morning arrive on your doorstep later that evening is a powerful persuader. But believing that convenience is the only decision factor is underestimating an emotional environment's competitive advantage.

In an effort to bring consumers back, retailers would do well to take a page out of Carlos' book and provide what the Internet cannot, environments that emotionally connect with consumers, consciously and subconsciously.

This environmental influence is the traditional retailer's strongest advantage against the cyber giants of online shopping.

But environment does have one limitation. It can't dramatically shorten the natural purchase cycle. For that, the lions in the grass have turned to something else—emotional obsolescence.

CHAPTER 16

EMOTIONAL OBSOLESCENCE

THE DASHBOARD'S LITTLE RED OILCAN LIGHT started to flash. Seconds later, we were coasting in silence to the side of the road.

Broke down in the middle of nowhere, far from cell phone coverage. Not a great start to our vacation.

I lifted the hood. Just as I thought, there was no glaring problem, no big "fix it" switch to be flipped. Only a shiny engine staring back at me.

I know a little about cars, but under the hood of these new vehicles, it's a mystery. There's not a spark plug, carburetor or fuel filter in sight.

Partly to satisfy the dash light warning, and partly because it was all I could do, I pulled the dipstick and checked the oil. It was low, but still registering between the indicator marks.

Shutting the hood, I looked through the windshield and offered my best "it'll be fine" smile. My wife didn't buy it.

We considered our options, and none were appealing—walk for hours or stay put and flag down a passing vehicle.

We sat in silence for what seemed like forever. Finally, with nothing to lose, I decided to just turn the key—and the big engine started! Our excitement was short-lived, though—with barely enough power to make the hills, we limped towards the next town.

AFTER A LITTLE EFFORT TO FIND A PHONE and an hour-long tow truck ride, I stood in front of a mechanic explaining what happened. He nodded and told us to come back tomorrow.

The next day, he informed us that the diagnostics showed no issues other than oil pressure.

"Good?" I asked, momentarily hopeful.

"No. Bad. It means your issue is internal. These big Chrysler engines have a small oil screen inside. If it gets plugged, sensors shut off the oil supply to the engine. To change it, I'd need to tear your engine apart."

"I see," I said, not seeing at all, but recognizing the reality of being five hours from home, having no working vehicle and feeling like this was about to get expensive. "Can you fix it?"

"To be honest, it'll be cheaper for you to buy a new engine. Too bad your warranty period just ended—it's like they build these to fail at a certain mileage. I don't know why Chrysler even put in this filter system." Then he added one final dagger. "These engines aren't built to last."

His words hung in the air like a cartoon speech bubble.

"… *just past your warranty period … fail at a certain mileage … aren't built to last …*"

The mechanic may not have known why these engines were designed this way, but I do. It's called **planned obsolescence**. It's a consumer strategy that is now built into most things, like cheap home-office printers with ink cartridges that cost as much as the whole printer, and cell phones that work great until the company launches the next version.

While it's reasonable to assume the manufacturers could identify defects and issues and sort them out, the truth is, they don't want to. Because being good is just bad for business.

My grandfather used to say that things weren't built like the old days. He realized new products were no longer built to last, but what he couldn't have understood back then is that this wasn't due to poor workmanship. This poor quality was intentional. Worse, this widely practiced strategy was specifically created to shorten the product replacement cycle.

It's planned obsolescence and it's effective because it's connected directly to our evolution.

THE EVOLUTION OF OUR DISSATISFACTION

GRANDDAD WAS RIGHT. Many of today's products are in fact not built like the "old days." Most are engineered to fail or be discarded long before most of their parts wear out. But however distasteful this engineered obsolescence may seem, it is aligned with our evolutionary instincts.

If Charles Darwin were around, he might explain our insatiable consumption and our need to upgrade most things in our lives as "just part of our evolutionary quest for survival." It's a process that's been ongoing ever since our single-celled ancestors slithered from the antediluvian sludge. But as sharp as Darwin was, he might not have connected this phenomenon with marketing.

Back when our basic survival meant competing with other species for limited resources, not picking fruit or taking possession of an empty cave at the precise moment it became available could mean someone or something else would—and that was a lost opportunity that could mean surviving or not.

This intensified human desire for immediate reward and heightened our fear of loss. Along the way, it also created a bottomless bucket of longing that we attempt to fill through today's equivalent of hunting and gathering, consumerism.

The instinct to improve our situation started long before we walked upright and still drives our desire to acquire today. Our search for reward (improvement) and constant effort to minimize threat (loss) is coded into our genes. It also explains why we are so tolerant of engineered obsolescence, and so attracted to consumerism.

EVOLUTION + OBSOLESCENCE = CONSUMERISM

BUT AREN'T WE SUPPOSED TO BE MODERN HUMANS, fully evolved, logical and rational? So how is it that we can still be so easily persuaded to acquire much more than we need? Have we always been consumed by consumerism?

Beyond food and shelter, why is it we need to buy bigger, better, more? When did we develop this unquenchable thirst for "stuff" beyond the essentials? (One look at the boot and shoe collection in our home and you'll understand the depth of my question.)

So what, or more accurately who, is to blame for our ravenous consumerism?

It's Franklin D. Roosevelt's fault.

Well, not exactly his fault. It's more like FDR's call to prepare for World War II and his necessary efforts to ready a nation for battle ignited an insatiable need to buy, spend, acquire and own. It was this call that ultimately led to obsolescence.

Please allow me to explain.

In 1939, Germany's military machine quickly pushed across Poland, the Netherlands and into France. Hitler's Blitzkrieg rolled through Europe with a speed and savage brutality that took even the most prepared countries by surprise.

German tanks and armored military vehicles supported by planes and mobile artillery led infantry through enemy positions faster than any army had ever advanced before as they pushed to occupy the coastlines.

Conquering Britain would have allowed the German war machine to cut off Allied supplies and realize a critical objective—capturing and controlling the Royal Navy, the world's most formidable armada.

On the other side of the Atlantic, Roosevelt had two main challenges: to pull his nation from the Great Depression that had reduced productivity to historically low levels and keep America from the conflict of yet another war on foreign soil.

FDR also realized that if Britain fell, it would only be a matter of time before the war in Europe was on his doorstep. Worse, he knew his nation wasn't ready.

In *Freedom's Forge,* the Pulitzer Prize-nominated author Arthur Herman describes how Winston Churchill's wartime telegram to Roosevelt warned that if Germany was successful against the Brits, they could commandeer the Royal Navy. The greatest single armed force in the world could be positioned off America's Atlantic shore in a matter of months.

Roosevelt's army chief of staff, General George Marshall, advised that America didn't have enough soldiers, tanks or machine guns to fight off an attack. If just five German divisions were to land on the coast, he concluded, German soldiers could go anywhere they wished in America. This got Roosevelt's attention.

Herman explains that, in the years following WW1, America's military force had been reduced from the world's fourth largest down to eighteenth, just ahead of tiny Holland. The United States Air Force consisted of approximately 1,700 planes, mostly fighters and trainers, while Hitler's Luftwaffe had built nearly 8,500 fighters and bombers at the outset of war.

FDR was convinced that Hitler's world domination aims included North America. But with the nation fighting to survive food shortages, spiraling economies and mass unemployment, what could be done?

Herman describes how Roosevelt motivated the nation, starting with America's most powerful businessmen. He reshaped the country into an industrial behemoth that was ultimately responsible for producing two-thirds of all Allied military equipment used in the war.

Factories were refitted with automation and new technology, and America, motivated by a unified purpose (and an emotional devil), began to manufacture and produce at incredible volumes.

Eventually the war ended. But the lessons in hyperproduction had laid the path for prosperity and intense economic growth.

Postwar optimism, new investment, the Employment Act of 1946 and billions in matured war bonds combined to create a new enterprise culture. The result was an exponential increase in the production of goods.

As the 1950s drew closer, American manufacturers needed to escalate consumer demand in order to keep up with production. For this they turned to the lions in the grass: the men and women made famous in *Mad Men*. They turned to influencers and persuaders to convince us that hyper-consumerism was culturally desirable behavior.

CONSUMERISM GETS EMOTIONAL

BEFORE THE WAR, merchandizing differentiated products by highlighting characteristics such as quality and durability. Consumers made decisions based on comparable facts and rational consideration of a product's quality, lifespan and functionality as guides in their purchasing process.

Post war, an abundance of products and purchasing options flooded the market. Consumer culture was on the verge of change.

As supply eclipsed demand, marketing began to transform from rational to emotional. Marketers moved away from common sense and spoke to their audience's hearts and dreams. And as consumerism became more culturally acceptable, lifestyle aspirations developed into the persuasion nucleus.

With more lifestyle opportunities, product options and disposable income available than ever before, behavior began to change. Consumerism became a way of life and a measurement of social status.

Marketers identifying this newly accepted culture began to position even the dullest domestic items as an emotional connection to a better life.

Enter the new marketing, linked to social status enhancement. With it, a new generation of persuaders emerged. Industry leaders and marketing agencies began to hire psychologists and invest in the prediction of human behavior.

The North American market had grown to become the largest in the world, but still supply outpaced demand. It was time for something drastic.

STRATEGIC OBSOLESCENCE

MANY HISTORIANS BELIEVE the transformation of North America into a consumer culture began before the start of the 19th century, but few would argue that hyper-consumerism didn't gain critical momentum until after World War II.

Following a decade of depression and years of war ration restrictions, Americans welcomed the change; they became preoccupied with the freedom connected to materialism. But it wasn't just persuaders pushing the population towards hyper-consumption. The urge to purchase was intensified by a government that equated consumerism with patriotism in an effort to enhance the national economy. The result: North Americans had money to spend, seemingly endless purchase options and could consume guilt-free—a patriotic way to serve self-interest.

The number of shopping centers in the U.S. increased from eight in 1945 to 3,840 just 15 years later.

As America embraced and then exported consumerism, obsolescence became the answer for manufacturers racing to intensify demand. Reengineering product durability from long-term to temporary became mainstream in an all-out effort to supply this new culture with more of everything.

In the mid 1950s, planned obsolescence was described by the industrial designer Brooks Stevens as "instilling in the buyer the desire to own something a little newer, a little better, a little sooner than is necessary."

For persuaders, these were the salad days as they appealed to this social force with innovative ways to generate additional spending. From vacuums to vehicles, styles changed, colors trended, and a revolving temporariness, usually reserved for the fashion industry, infiltrated every aspect of the economy.

What couldn't be reengineered for functional obsolescence became the focus of emotional obsolescence.

As manufacturers faced the reality that some products didn't wear out fast enough, they looked to the persuader's ability to emotionally manipulate the life cycle of desirability. Emotional obsolescence was born.

By simultaneously evoking dissatisfaction with the products we owned and psychologically elevating the value of their replacements, purchase cycles were shortened dramatically.

For persuaders, the new strategy was seen as a win-win. If a product broke down because of a function failure, then the problem would be linked directly to the manufacturer. But if the owner became disenchanted with their current product and desired the updated model, then their decision was not a result of poor manufacturing. In fact, by purchasing the latest model, the consumer displayed their freedom and status.

By introducing new rationales that lowered consumers' emotional commitment to their recent purchase, manufacturers could wear out a product's desirability well before its functionality wore out.

This approach is evident in the 1950s auto industry, where marketing implied that people who regularly upgraded to new vehicle models were intellectually superior to those who didn't, due to their understanding of the lifestyle value of a new car.

Using this approach, persuaders further expanded consumerism by emotionally connecting their audience's perception of health, safety, freedom and status as reasons to upgrade.

In the 1960 book *The Waste Makers*, author Vance Packard presents the example of Chevrolet's ads communicating to *"those deprived citizens who were victims of one-car captivity."* The message was designed to emotionally influence families into feeling they were suffering from the entrapment of having only one car.

As the 1950s advanced, persuaders combined planned obsolescence with emotional presentation. Most products fit with the planned obsolescence strategy, and those that couldn't be engineered to fail were reinvented and presented as "new and improved."

One classic example is the refrigerator. Realizing the deeply negative consequences of purposefully engineering functionally obsolescent fridges, manufacturers turned to the fashion industry. Using emotional obsolescence to lead owners towards disenchantment with their existing models, they convinced consumers to trade in their perfect working appliances for the modern styles, features and color options of new models. Enter: avocado appliances and pink bathroom furnishings.

Emotional and functional obsolescence has become an accepted part of our culture and is now found in most persuasion strategies. But the persuader's ability to use emotion to influence the behavior of individuals pales in comparison to the dark art of mass manipulation and the power to control crowds now reaching its apex.

"Madness is rare in individuals—but in groups, parties, nations, and ages it is the rule."

Friedrich Nietzsche 1844 – 1900

CHAPTER 17

THE EMOTIONAL MADNESS OF CROWDS

WELCOME, FIGHT FANS ...

On a cool November evening in Las Vegas, Riddick Bowe and Evander Holyfield sat quietly in their dressing rooms preparing for the 1993 heavyweight title fight.

Billed as "Repeat or Revenge," this was a grudge match between two fighters who hated each other. Every person packed into the outdoor stadium knew it.

The fighters entered the ring, touched gloves and for seven consecutive rounds the crowd roared as Bowe and Holyfield traded punches, attempting to inflict as much physical damage as possible.

Suddenly, the two fighters froze. Confused, they stared into the night sky. A paraglider plummeted towards them.

With a motorized fan strapped to his back, James Miller descended from the dark and crash-landed into the ropes. His parachute was caught overhead in the lights while he dangled like a marionette, bouncing between the ring and the crowd.

Then, chaos.

Fans, trainers and security guards tore at the ensnared paraglider, punching, kicking and pounding him into unconsciousness. The few who tried to stop the madness were pushed aside. The crowd, now a single-minded mass, acted with only one intention, to attack the intruder.

Finally the beatings stopped, and the unconscious Miller was pulled from his motorized rig and rushed from the ring. Spectators scrambled to pull down his parachute, ripping and slashing it into pieces for souvenirs.

It didn't seem real.

Later Miller would say, "It was a heavyweight fight and I was the only guy who got knocked out."

Watching from home, far from the crowd's descent into madness, I stared at the bizarre event. What just happened? Was it a promotion? A stunt? Did his engine fail? And why the hell were the spectators beating that guy? The questions reeled as I watched the crowd, driven by some unseen unifying force, attack without hesitation. It was as if someone somewhere flipped a switch. What had driven a diverse group of unconnected individuals into a collectively violent madness?

Tangled in the ropes, Miller posed no threat. His decision to achieve his 15 minutes of fame at the cost of the boxing fans' concentration was questionable, but it wasn't malicious intent to injure.

He simply crashed the wrong party.

Landing in an environment where elements had combined to create a potentially explosive state, Miller became the spark that ignited a fuse. He was an unrelated ingredient that tipped the crowd from individual rationality into aligned insanity.

Later that night, walking out of the arena, it's likely the aggressors wondered what the hell had drawn them into the crowd and why they had acted so irrationally.

But it was predictable. And persuaders use the crowd's behavior to manipulate individuals—all the time.

THE UNCONSCIOUS ATTRACTION OF CROWDS

I KNOW WHAT YOU'RE THINKING. "The herd mentality has no impact on me. I'm a logical person, a rational thinker."

You could be right. That is, if your version of the mob is an unruly crowd acting as a destructive force, kicking over police barricades and smashing store windows.

It's a popular interpretation, but it's not the typical one. While these mad mobs do erupt, it is the rarity rather than the norm. Whether we realize it or not, in almost every aspect of life, our behavior is unconsciously altered by the magnetic power of crowds. And this is absolutely natural.

Our need to follow a trend, listen to an influencer, dress "in style" or agree with the majority is less about our needs and more about our preprogrammed association with **conformity**.

Be it counting the likes on our latest post or buying home decorating magazines to define our own style, we instinctually "herd" without knowing it.

Our emotional compass guides us at a subconscious level to join groups, update our wardrobe, fit in, and connect with like-minded individuals. Even those revolting against conformity find emotional solace in the company of similarly minded (and dressed) individuals.

In Don Norman's 2005 book *Emotional Design: Why We Love (or Hate) Everyday Things*, he states that "the emotional side of design may be more critical to a product's success than its practical elements. Emotions are inseparable from, and a necessary part of, cognition."

As a cognitive scientist and a former vice president of Apple, Norman may know a thing or two about what dictates our behavior. "Everything we do, everything we think is tinged with emotion, much of it subconscious," he explains.

Our subconscious ensures that we don't stray from the crowd because that is where we are the most protected.

SAFETY IN NUMBERS

As the lady in red who appeared at the beginning of the book said, "All these people can't be wrong." We often exchange our self-direction for the herd mentality and rely on the recommendations of complete strangers who may even be fictitiously created. (Yes, "Bob from Kansas" who left a five-star rating for the useless coffee maker I just bought, I'm talking to you.)

While no one sees themselves as part of a mob, most if not all of us regularly migrate towards the herd and conform to its opinion whether we realize it or not.

Perhaps it was trying the Zone or Keto Diet. Maybe it was drinking carb-free beer (guilty as charged … *sigh*) or switching to aspartame.

We remain steadfast in our belief that the herd's influence has little effect upon us, yet evidence to the contrary is everywhere.

Consider the dramatic changes we undergo in something as firmly established as our collective appreciation of what we find attractive in the opposite sex.

For most men in the 1920s, the ideal female form included a boyish body style and short hair, with clothing cut to flatten chests and eliminate curves. By the 1930s, curves were making a comeback. By the 1950s, the epitome of female beauty was Marilyn Monroe's hourglass figure, which appealed to the masses until the '60s, when tall, thin models like Twiggy represented sexual desirability.

Twenty years later healthy, athletic builds were attracting the masses, until the 1990s, when we were persuaded to buy products by gaunt models in an era the fashion industry referred to as Heroin Chic.

Today the dark ringed eyes and pale thin bodies that were attractive in the 1990s are considered unhealthy. Athletic builds with accentuated breasts and butts and impossibly thin waistlines now influence our current opinion of beauty. Can you imagine someone in the '90s asking for an injection of hydrogel for a buttocks augmentation?

The basic human form hasn't changed in millions of years, yet our collective opinion of what is attractive changes regularly.

The hourglass-shaped female movie stars of the '50s would hardly conform to what most of today's young men find attractive. And watching the leading men of that era strut shirtless across the silver screen with beltlines hiked above their navel would leave most of today's women asking, "Where's the beef?"

Changes in our attraction are influenced by how others react, whether it's preferring one brand over another or a certain body shape. As trends grow in momentum, their allure increases exponentially. The larger the crowd that follows a trend, the more appealing it becomes.

Want proof of our need to follow the crowd? Just look at a photo of yourself dressed up 25 years ago. Chances are more than a few things have changed since then. Looking back, perhaps like me you question your sanity, wondering what convinced you to dress in that double-breasted, triple-shoulder-padded suit and wear that hairstyle. Damn you, Duran Duran. Damn you, Flock of Seagulls. Damn you, conformity.

Even though our preference for a style, fashion or trend may feel like our own, it is, as scientists have discovered, an unconscious decision made to increase our potential for survival.

Recent studies have revealed that individuals subconsciously adjust their judgments of what is attractive in order to conform to the group's opinion. It turns out, this is more than just trying to fit in—we are chemically guided to conform.

In a 2010 study, scientists Daniel Campbell-Meiklejohn, Dominik Bach, Chris Frith, Andreas Roepstorff and Ray Dolan investigated social conformity and how the opinions of others affect our own.

Using functional magnetic resonance imaging, they studied how the brain reacts during a decision to conform and agree with others about the value of an object even despite conflicting evidence. They discovered that when agreeing with others, our brain produces activity in a region of the ventral striatum. **This brain activity is similar to the neural reward experienced when receiving an object we desire.**

In short, neuroscience proves that we are chemically compensated for conforming to the opinion of others.

Scientist Vasily Klucharev, the director of the Institute of Cognitive Neuroscience in Moscow, also explored this concept. His laboratory studies revealed that changing one's opinion to match the group's when under social influence triggers a massive dopamine release in the brain.

Klucharev found that, by temporarily suppressing the brain's dopamine response, he could reverse and reduce his subject's desire to conform to the group's opinion by a massive 40 percent.

Klucharev believes that we are not even aware of the majority's influence on our behavior, stating, "We need to understand how easily we can be manipulated because of the way our brain has been shaped by evolution." He argues that "Being a conformist may be right from a biological and evolutionary point of view … Human behavior patterns have been tested by evolution, and this one has proven to be effective, because we have survived and continue to procreate."

In Denmark, another experiment was conducted to see if the desire to conform could be influenced externally. By giving volunteers a pill that increased the amount of dopamine in the brain, the test subjects were observed to change their minds more readily to match the majority opinion.

These results again demonstrate how we are chemically rewarded when we conform.

This research suggests what persuaders practicing the dark art of manipulation already know: Our need to conform is instinctual. It's also elevated by our perception of the crowd's size.

AN EXCELLENT EXAMPLE IS SOCIAL MEDIA. Our opinions are enhanced by our perception of the number of followers an influencer has as much as by the influencers themselves. The more followers they have, the more contagious they are.

The other action-triggering component is the audience's emotional relationship with this influencer. We may follow someone just because everyone else is, but if we feel a personal connection, we are even more inclined to act upon his or her direction.

This is why the selection of the right spokespeople can have such a positive or negative persuasive impact on an advertiser's brand.

If you're not a Matthew McConaughey fan, regardless of his follower numbers, your dopamine levels won't be altered by his appearance in Cadillac's commercials. *"Alright, alright, alright."* You won't be inclined to act.

Whether it's safety in numbers, survival-based, evolutionarily directed, a dopamine reward or an instinctual fear of missing out—unconsciously we adopt the behavior of the herd. And just as the raindrop doesn't know it's part of the flood, we conform and collectively begin to influence others.

But this need to conform isn't our fault. After all, we inherited it.

THE EVOLUTION OF CONFORMITY

OUR EARLIEST ANCESTORS LEARNED HARD LESSONS on the pros and cons of conformity. Together the tribe hunted, prospered and survived. Conforming to the group was a rational choice. Failing to conform could mean being cast out to attempt to survive alone.

SURVIVAL OF THE FITTEST?
SURVIVAL OF THE CONFORMIST.

IMAGINE A SMALL TRIBE of our prehistoric ancestors. Standing upright, peering over the savanna's grassy plains, surveying the horizon for any creature straying from its pack. Rocks and spears ready, adrenaline flowing, they spot the lone animal and collectively attack as a single-minded group.

It is highly likely that this was adaptive learning, watching others and observing natural predators hunt—experiences that surely influenced our primitive development.

Each experience reinforced the fact that those outside of the pack didn't last long, while those within it did.

To conform = life

To not conform = death

No one wants to believe they **need** interdependence but our urge to conform socially in order to connect and interact within the group is hardwired into our DNA.

Matthew Lieberman, a scientist and director of the social cognitive neuroscience lab at UCLA, is the author of *Social: Why Our Brains Are Wired to Connect.*

In a 2013 *Scientific American* magazine interview, Lieberman said, "We may not like the fact that we are wired such that our well-being depends on our connections with others, but the facts are the facts."

Lieberman believes that threats to our survival are received as social discomfort (rejection) that causes actual pain. He also believes that the existence of social pain is a sign evolution has made social connection a necessity, not a luxury.

If you are reading this, it's a safe bet that you're a descendent of those who conformed as a group to survive against hungry predators, rival tribes and anyone or anything pursuing the lone and vulnerable. It is also reasonable to assume that you've unconsciously conformed to the opinion of others—and that professional persuaders have manipulated this characteristic.

Don't believe me? Grab that 25-year-old photo of yourself again.

This instinctual necessity to conform is still prevalent today. We align with like-minded people to create our modern-day tribes and we react differently when infected with a crowd's energy. How loud would you cheer in a stadium if you were alone in the stands?

Evolution reinforced conformity. Now it's an unconscious reaction. It has become perfectly rational to buy according to the five-star ratings of complete strangers, to follow the latest trends and buy the latest fashions. After all, to conform is to survive.

This hardwiring has also made us vulnerable, however. Persuaders leverage conformation tactics to manipulate the masses and control our behavior. From Cabbage Patch dolls to the latest iPhone, our ephemeral desire-to-acquire often has less to do with our personal thoughts on a product and more to do with what others think about it.

The daunting question: if this evolutionary trait can be manipulated to influence our minor decisions, are we also susceptible to a persuader's tactics on large-scale decisions and behavior?

Unfortunately, the answer is yes.

CONFORMITY'S PERSUASIVE POWER

THE FRENZIED LOOK ON THE FACES of those pressed against the glass waiting for the Black Friday sale to begin is a small but fitting example of persuasion's power.

Despite the employees' terror on the retail side of the flexing store windows, outside, the hair-pulling, line-butting, shoving, pushing and general raging madness isn't a surprise. This controlled chaos is going exactly as someone planned.

Waiting for hours and risking a trampling death to save $89 on a soon-to-be-outdated PVR may seem like a self-directed decision to those in line. It is actually a result of premeditated emotional manipulation. It is how persuaders start by enticing individuals to corral as a group, then use the crowd itself to attract others and finally to guide people away from their own identity and exchange it for the group's personality.

Emotional manipulation combined with crowd consciousness generates irrational but predictable behavior and enables persuaders to influence the emotions of crowds.

Like a stadium of sports fans in costumes or with proudly painted torsos cheering at an earsplitting volume, individual behavior is magnified by the actions of others.

The good news is that the heightened effect of this influence is temporary. Individual thought will return in time. The bad news is that when it does return, you might just be sitting in traffic dressed as a devil or a dolphin.

NEARLY A CENTURY BEFORE BEHAVIORAL SCIENTISTS discovered that the human brain released large amounts of dopamine to reward us for conforming, the French scientist Charles-Marie Gustave Le Bon wrote *The Crowd: A Study of the Popular Mind.*

Gustave Le Bon described the contagiousness of crowds and explained that evidence, truth or error in a crowd's opinion have little consequence. When a crowd believes something, the individuals within it accept the belief without question. Le Bon cited the Crusaders who believed they saw an image of Saint George on the walls of Jerusalem. *"By dint of suggestion and contagion the miracle signalized by a single person was immediately accepted by all,"* he wrote.

Le Bon compared the transformation from individual to a mindless part of a mass to chemistry: *"... Just as in chemistry certain elements, when brought into contact—bases and acids, for example—combine to form a new body possessing properties quite different from those of the bodies that have served to form it."*

Whether it's feeling the contagiousness of a crowd's energy or accepting others' opinions over our own, we are hardwired to conform.

THE PERSUASION OF SOCIAL CONFORMITY

RESTAURATEURS FILL THEIR WINDOW SEATS FIRST. It's not for the benefit of the patrons inside—it's the outsiders looking in they wish to influence. Because we trust the actions and opinions of others, if the restaurant looks full, well, chances are it must be good.

Behavioral scientists call adopting the opinion of others in order to socially conform "deindividualization."

Group size, environmental influence and emotional relevance all affect the depth of deindividualization, how far someone descends into the crowd's identity.

To experience this, the next time you're in a crowded environment such as a mall or a busy sidewalk, stop and pretend to photograph an object. This will result in little more than grumbling as you disturb the traffic flow. But try it again, this time with several friends in a group all pointing cameras at the same object. The impact and interest generated among those passing by will be exponentially related to the number of photographers you have focused on the subject.

This conformity tactic is well known to professional persuaders, who use it in marketing language every day.

"We are painting houses in your neighborhood. Let us know if you would like a free quote."

OR:

"Call this number to receive a free house painting quote."

"This hotel room leads in number of guests concerned about saving the planet and reusing their towels."

OR:

"Please help save our planet. Reuse your towels."

"Get out the vote."

OR:

"Get out the vote, a record turnout is expected."

One approach influences action by leveraging our unconscious need for conformity and inclusion. The other simply makes a statement.

If creating a group environment isn't an option, persuaders can still create a **virtual crowd** through repetition. If something is relevant and repeated by enough people, we tend to accept it into our belief system regardless of its validity.

As such, many of our opinions are not our opinions at all. We hear a rumor or even a jingle enough times from enough sources and it becomes part of our default belief system.

"It ain't what you don't know that gets you into trouble. It's what you know for sure that just ain't so.[5]"

» *Shaving makes hair grow back thicker.* I have bald friends who shave their heads daily and would contest this.

» *We use only 10 percent of our brains.* Nope, research shows activity all over our cranial mass.

» *Baby Jesus was visited by three Wise Men.* Nope. No specific number is indicated anywhere in the Bible, and staying on topic, Adam didn't bite into an apple in the Garden of Eden. According to the Book of Genesis, he chomped into an unspecified forbidden fruit.

» *When attacked by a grizzly bear, run downhill.* Sure, if you want to be its next meal. Grizzlies can travel up to 50 feet a second (almost 40 miles per hour) on almost all terrain. Even if their front legs are shorter than their hind legs and they happen to tumble, when the

---

5   A quote variously attributed to Mark Twain, Josh Billings and Will Rogers, among others.

somersaulting stops the grizzly can run back up the hill at a speed equal to most racehorses. So, maybe pick a new escape plan.

» *Bulls lose it when they see red.* Nope. They're color-blind, but they see the fabric the matador is waving as a threat.

While the knowledge needed to face a raging bull or stare down a grizzly may not be a daily necessity, the point is, we've adopted many of our opinions based on what we've heard repeatedly.

Much of our need to conform is based on a deep instinctual desire to survive, prosper and procreate. But adopting the opinions of others isn't just about conforming; it's about necessity, as we often have neither the time nor capacity to generate our own analyses.

In Dan Ariely's brilliant book *Predictably Irrational, The Hidden Forces That Shape Our Decisions,* he uses Leonardo da Vinci's *Mona Lisa* as an example of how our opinions come to us preformed. "For most of us the painting is beautiful and the smile is mysterious because we are told it is so," he writes. Ariely goes on to explain that in the absence of expertise or perfect information, we use social cues and the opinions of others to help us figure out how much we are, or should be, impressed. Our expectations take care of the rest.

It's instinctive for us to conform. It's also natural that we rely on others where our experience or our desire to learn falls short. We have no choice. Given the diverse and complex nature of our world, it is impossible to become expert in every field. From hiring a locksmith to understanding the art of the High Renaissance, to bullfighting, we need, conform to and rely upon the opinions of others. And it is this need that sits at the core of persuasion's influence.

Calls to action combining conformity with FOMO (Fear of Missing Out) may be more or less harmless. (*Everyone else is buying, so get yours today! Subscribe now and join our exclusive group of insiders!*) But this base tactic can be ratcheted up by master persuaders to generate an ominous new level of manipulation.

This level of persuasion becomes a danger when the people holding positions of authority wield these tactics for personal gain at the expense of others. Then the influence goes beyond convincing shoppers to one-click their order on Amazon and becomes the ultimate persuasion weapon. Propaganda—the terrifyingly powerful manipulation of the masses.

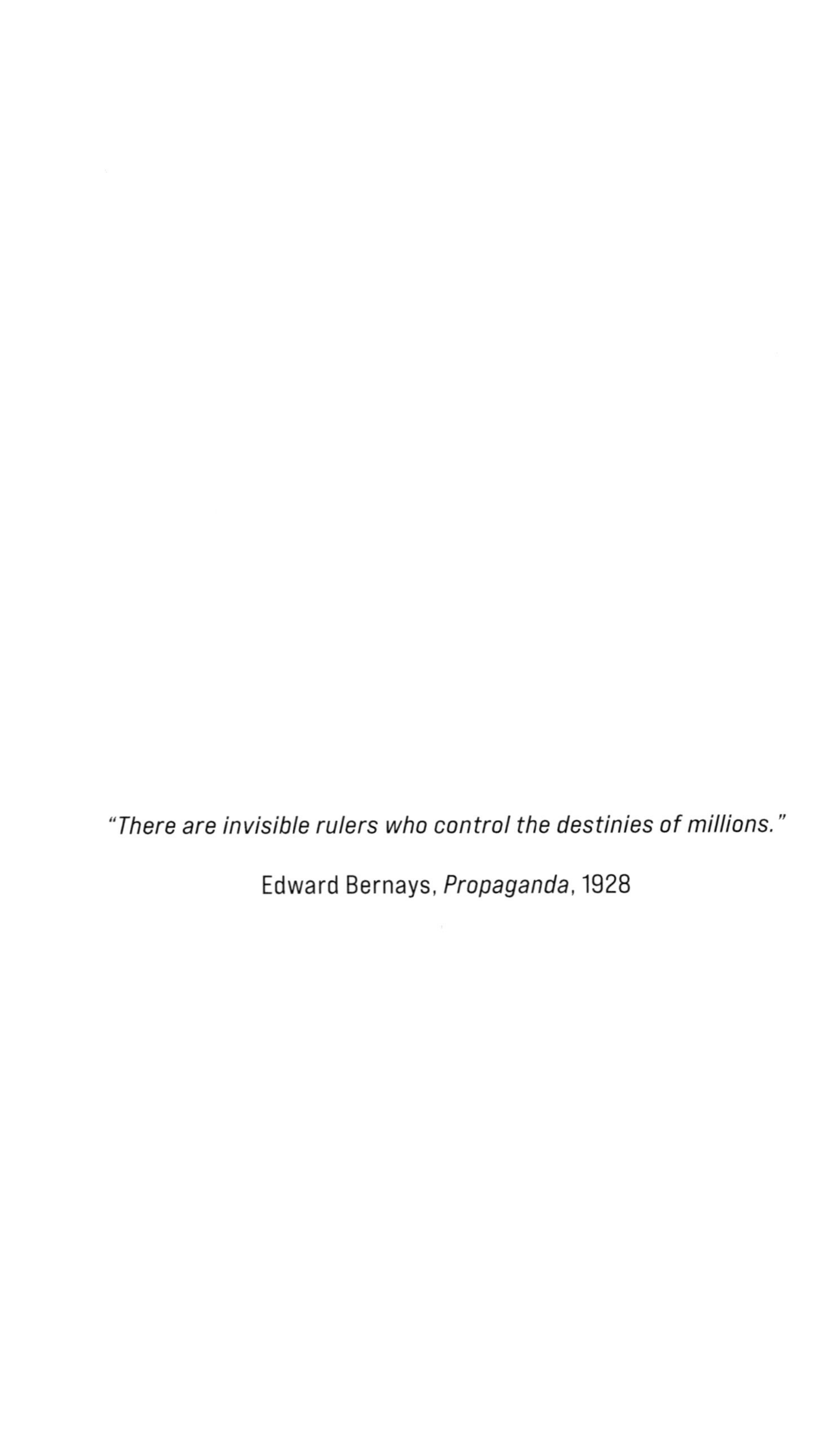

"There are invisible rulers who control the destinies of millions."

Edward Bernays, *Propaganda*, 1928

CHAPTER 18

PERSUADING A NATION

BEFORE WE GET INTO THE EMOTIONAL MANIPULATION of the masses, let's talk about something better. Bacon.

Yes, bacon. That high-fat and sodium-studded treat. Eggs' sidekick at breakfast, sandwiched between lettuce and tomatoes at lunch, scattered on baked potatoes at dinner and hanging out with pineapple chunks on pizza for late-night snacks. Somehow, bacon made its way from relative anonymity to playing a part in almost every meal.

Bacon has sizzled its way into our hearts, and every year the average North American consumes about 18 pounds. But our cultural bacon fixation didn't start until the mid-1920s, when the Beech-Nut Packing Company, whose main product was bacon in a jar, no less, hired Sigmund Freud's nephew, Edward Bernays.

In 1990, *Life Magazine* listed Bernays as one of the 100 most influential people in America in the prior century. But if you know of Edward

Bernays, you're among a select few. This relatively anonymous wizard of persuasion worked from behind the curtain to influence everything from what we eat to how we vote.

Bernays was definitely not the first professional persuader. But building on the work and reputation of his famous uncle Sigmund, he parlayed psychology, persuasion and propaganda to shape consumer culture on a multitude of things, including bringing back bacon. (Mmmm, back bacon!)

In the 1920s, North America's interest in the newly invented processed cereals was growing. Big breakfasts were exchanged for convenient dry cereals. Some even snapped, crackled and popped. And the Battle Creek Sanitarium Food Company (aka Kellogg's) took over the market.

Bacon's popularity was sliding. That is, until Bernays engineered a culture shift. By sending 5,000 letters through his own doctor, Bernays asked MDs across the country to respond to a simple question: Was it better to start the day with a light breakfast or a hearty breakfast?

The response was resounding—4,500 physicians responded that a hearty breakfast was better for the health of the American public. Bernays sent the results to journalists, newspapers and magazines. Soon headlines throughout the nation reported that "4,500 physicians agree that a hearty breakfast is the healthiest way to start the day."

Ads featuring bacon as an important part of a healthy breakfast appeared in newspapers and magazines, while editorial writers reported that a hearty breakfast was the healthy choice to feed your family. Focusing on the emotional desire to be healthy, Bernays connected the act of eating big breakfasts (featuring bacon) with the benefits of a good lifestyle. It was a classic example of using our need to conform and rely on the opinion of others.

From the "All American Breakfast" to Wendy's Baconator cheeseburger, our passion for the little carcinogenic, heart-stopping strips began with Bernays' influence over our emotions. Bacon may be delicious, but his marketing triumph had nothing to do with America's taste buds.

Beyond bacon, Bernays influenced everything from politics to culture. Working with large corporate clients like Proctor & Gamble and General Electric as well as presidential candidates Calvin Coolidge and Herbert Hoover, Bernays used emotional manipulation to influence public behavior.

In his 1928 book *Propaganda,* Bernays explains that to influence culture and consumerism on a grand scale, you first need to control the hidden influencer, human emotion.

While his uncle Sigmund exposed how the unconscious triggered emotion and controlled behavior, Bernays took these insights a step further.

By focusing on the preset beliefs of his audience and the evolutionary need to conform, Bernays used propaganda techniques to affect public opinion on everything from bacon to cigarettes to who should sit in the Oval Office.

He wasn't alone.

THE POWER OF MASS PERSUASION

POP QUIZ #1:

What century were these statements written? Bonus marks if you can identify the author.

"Advertising, in the field of business or of politics, will carry success by continuity and regular uniformity of application."

"All effective propaganda has to limit itself only to a very few points and to use them like slogans until (everyone) is able to imagine what is intended

by such a word … and each member of the public understands what you want him (or her) to understand by your slogan."

"What would one say about a poster, for instance, which was to advertise a new soap, and which nevertheless describes other soaps as 'also being good'? We would shake our heads."

If you guessed that these were written early in the last century, give yourself full marks! These statements are from Volume 1, Chapter Six of a book written in 1925 about, among other things, emotional mass control.

If you recognize these proclamations, you already understand the extreme danger of emotional mass manipulation and propaganda.

Even if you don't know the quotes, you may recognize the book's title, *Mein Kampf* (*My Fight*), by Adolf Hitler.

Mein Kampf details Hitler's ideology and thoughts on achieving a new world order by controlling public perception with propaganda and emotional mass manipulation.

About the same time the Nazis were invading Poland, George Orwell, who had a thought or two on the terrifying possibilities of a dystopian future, got his hands on a copy of *Mein Kampf.* He warned England not to underestimate Hitler and to ready itself for an attack. His predictions about life in 1984 may not have been 100 percent accurate, but he was bang on in his assessment of Hitler's plan. (Orwell's *1984* sales skyrocketed to become Amazon's overall number one-selling book just days after Trump's inauguration.)

As Gustave Le Bon said in 1896, *"These leaders are often subtle rhetoricians, seeking only their own personal interest, and endeavoring to persuade by flattering base instincts."*

THE FUNDAMENTALS OF MASS MANIPULATION

WHEN FACING THREAT, we instinctively turn tribal. It is our evolutionary advantage, bringing individuals into group cohesion. Tribes work together, be it hunting or fighting other tribes. But fear has also been weaponized as a method of control.

Since the dawn of civilization, persuaders have introduced a vague threat to trigger a collective focus on survival. Thus manipulated, even the most independent individuals adopt the views of the masses.

From Pope Urban's 1000 AD Crusades-motivating speech describing Muslims as *murderers of Christians, violent torturers of men* and *ravishers of women*; to George W. Bush's *Weapons of Mass Destruction*; to Kennedy's *Missile Gap*; to Trump describing refugees as *illegal aliens, criminals, rapists and murderers*; audience unification is achieved by identifying (or creating) and then amplifying a relevant threat to our survival. Naturally, the threat is one that only the persuaders can save us from.

No survival = No Procreation = No Existence

When fear is introduced, we rely on our instincts, unifying to work together in a collective effort to survive.

Our evolution-guided actions are dominated by the need to conform.

When you hear the fire alarm at work, do you get up and run for the doors? Or is your first instinct to look around and see how everyone else is reacting?

When fear is evoked by a figure of authority who we believe is acting on our behalf, such as an elected official, we become hyper-responsive. This is the core of propaganda.

Real and perceived threats **are experienced the same way**, so even the potential of threat can spike our evolutionary instincts. Consider how many world-ending catastrophic threats we have been presented with that never came to fruition in the last 20 years alone. Y2K comes to mind: market crashes, global blackouts, planes dropping from the sky at the precise minute our calendar changed. The antidote: invest heavily in technology. Heavily. The Cold War, weapons of mass destruction, the axis of evil, communism, socialism, and so on.

In this constant state of survival-conformity, we are more likely to adopt the opinion of the masses and become more manageable (read as **manipulatable**). Even if the threat is unfounded and we **suspect** the persuader is using it to achieve their own personal agenda—say, to get reelected—our evolutionary response kicks in and we look to the masses for guidance.

Because potential threat is experienced as real, using fear to jeopardize any level of our survival is a powerful motivator. Whether it's fear of death, disease, terrorists, loss, exclusion, nuclear attack, violent dictators or volatile politicians, threats to our survival magnify our need to conform.

Ultimately, this enables the manipulation of the masses and propels a culture of fear.

THE CULTURE OF FEAR

"… the only thing we have to fear is fear itself…."

PRESIDENT FRANKLIN D. ROOSEVELT SPOKE these memorable words in his 1933 inaugural speech to the American public during the Depression. FDR understood the ability of fear to reach beyond race, culture and status, and its potentially devastating effect on the entire nation.

FDR was an emotional revolutionary (more on that later) and believed people shouldn't live in fear. Unfortunately, many following in his presidential footsteps have rejected this approach. Instead, using threat-based propaganda techniques, they have leveraged fear to achieve personal and political agendas.

Frank Furedi, a former professor of sociology and the author of *Politics of Fear: Beyond Left and Right*, believes fear shapes culture, and populations existing in a climate of fear become vulnerable to their government's increased control.

Adam Curtis agrees. In his BBC documentary series *The Power of Nightmares, The Rise of the Politics of Fear*, Curtis argues that politicians increase their power through propaganda by positioning an organized threat as something that (only) they can protect us from.

The good news is that once we see these propaganda patterns, in both politics and marketing, we can reduce our vulnerability to their manipulation.

WAR ON TERROR, PATTERNS OF PROPAGANDA

PROPAGANDA FOLLOWS A SET PATTERN. It begins as a mutual and wide threat, slowly narrowing into an emotionally relevant survival-threatening inevitability.

The steps? Pick a devil and describe it as a threat to world safety. Support this with information. Then, modify the threat to become personally relevant to the audience. Introduce the opinion of experts. Amplify the threat as unavoidable. Give it a timeline. Detail the only solution: a collective action against this devil.

Consider Iraq and the "weapons of mass destruction." While the threat was presented over time, transcripts of President Bush's October 2002 speech present a perfect example of propaganda's pattern.

The point here isn't to debate the reality of the threat, only to identify the presentation process, patterns and propaganda tactics.

Step One: Identify the devil, present the threat, position it as a world-wide issue.

"We agree that the Iraqi dictator must not be permitted to threaten America and the world with horrible poisons, and diseases, and gases, and atomic weapons.

"Iraq's weapons of mass destruction are controlled by a murderous tyrant, who has already used chemical weapons to kill thousands of people.

"(Saddam Hussein) ... has struck other nations without warning and holds an unrelenting hostility towards the United States.

"Saddam Hussein is a homicidal dictator who is addicted to weapons of mass destruction."

Step Two: Make it real, support it with information and articulate the threat.

"If we know Saddam Hussein has dangerous weapons today—and we do—does it make any sense for the world to wait to confront him as he grows even stronger and develops even more dangerous weapons?

"This is a massive stockpile of biological weapons that has never been accounted for and is capable of killing millions. We know that the regime has produced thousands of tons of chemical agents."

Step Three: Modify the threat to make it personally relevant to your audience.

"Iraq is exploring ways of using UAVs (Unmanned Aerial Vehicles – remotely piloted aircraft) for missions targeting the United States.

"Iraq could decide on any given day to provide a biological or chemical weapon to a terrorist group or individual terrorists."

Step Four: Introduce expert opinions.

"(Before the Gulf War) inspectors discovered that Iraq had an advanced nuclear weapons development program, had a design for a workable nuclear weapon, and was pursuing several different methods of enriching uranium for a bomb."

Step Five: Amplify the threat as imminent.

"The evidence indicates that Iraq is reconstituting its nuclear weapons program.

"Saddam Hussein has held numerous meetings with Iraqi nuclear scientists, a group he calls his nuclear mujahedeen—his nuclear holy warriors."

Step Six: Give the threat a defined timeline.

"If the Iraqi regime is able to produce, buy or steal an amount of highly-enriched uranium a little larger than a single softball, it could have a nuclear weapon in less than a year."

Step Seven: Detail the solution, a collective action against the devil.

"Knowing these realities, America must not ignore the threat gathering against us.

"Facing clear evidence of peril, we cannot wait for the final proof—the smoking gun—that could come in the form of a mushroom cloud.

"We have every reason to assume the worst, and we have an urgent duty to prevent the worst from occurring."

The final propaganda tactic is to eliminate opposition before it gains momentum. By identifying those who disagree, persuaders use conformity to position those in opposition as being part of the problem. In this case, Bush identified these people and nations as weak-minded, unpatriotic sympathizers:

"You are either with us, or with the terrorists."
George W. Bush

Whether Iraq's weapons of mass destruction were real or a fabrication, the threat was presented in a pattern proven to trigger a specific evolutionary response.

To sell a war, identify a devil, frighten the people and offer a solution.

POP QUIZ #2:

Who was recorded saying this about the manipulation of a nation?

"Of course the people don't want war. But after all, it's the leaders of the country who determine the policy, and it's always a simple matter to drag the people along, whether it's a democracy, a fascist dictatorship, or a parliament, or a communist dictatorship. Voice or no voice, the people can always be brought to the bidding of the leaders. That's easy. All you have to do is tell them they're being attacked and denounce the pacifists for lack of patriotism and exposing the country to greater danger."

The answer:

Hermann Göring. Recorded April 18, 1946, in his cell during the Nuremberg trials.

Sophisticated persuaders understand that mass manipulation is achieved through communication control. This includes the type of message, its format and its distribution—and that means influencing the media.

At its core, propaganda's exploitive tactics follow a set pattern. But the source of its power is the ability to create a culture of fear by using short, memorable statements (as Hitler identified in *Mein Kampf*) designed specifically to become sound bites for the media and the masses.

Ultimately, when persuaders gain control over words and their distribution, they can control the people.

WHY PROPAGANDA SPREADS

THE MEDIA KNOWS THE AUDIENCE'S ATTENTION is connected to its survival instincts, which prioritizes the potentially harmful over the potentially positive. They know bad news outsells good.

This enables fear-trepreneurs to use each new threat to achieve their own aims, by manipulating the masses through media exposure.

Making matters worse (or better, depending on your position) is the threat echo. Media coverage fans the panic, as we experience the emotional fear of what **may happen** in full. Then, if a crisis actually comes to fruition, regardless of the size of its effect, the emotional reaction is exponential. And the media's "told you so" coverage presents a second wave.

Potential terrorism becomes news and coverage fans the panic. One person tries to wear a shoe bomb onto a plane and the threat echo results in a planet of sock-footed people shuffling through airport security holding up their beltless pants.

Crime, corruption, terrorism and gun violence. National debt and international threats. Famine, floods and forest fires. Market crashes, cold wars and climate changes. Pandemics, epidemics, endemics—any of the -demics, really. Bad news is good news, or at least a good opportunity for the media to capture the audience and sell advertising while persuaders manipulate emotions.

"The whole aim of practical politics is to keep the populace alarmed by an endless series of hobgoblins, most of them imaginary."
— H.L. Mencken, 1918

But not all propaganda tactics threaten the violent end of our survival. Some are cleverly aligned with our passionate beliefs about what is righteous and good, like our children's future, freedom of speech, or the environment. This is where the best persuaders employ the uber-power of propaganda to achieve their personal objectives.

THIS IS OFTEN HARDER TO DETECT. We filter incoming information through our predetermined biases. If what we receive supports what we already believe, the information is welcomed past our defenses like a Trojan horse, even though it is cleverly crafted to advance the persuaders' personal agendas.

The good news is that once you understand the patterns, even those using seemingly good intentions as emotional manipulation tactics become easier to spot.

Channel surfing a while back, I happened across a late-night talk show interview with then presidential candidate Bernie Sanders.

Aside from looking a little like a *Seinfeld* character, Sanders seemed to be relatively rational, or as rational as anyone running for president could be.

The key message he wove through the interview was the devastation of climate change—connecting it to droughts, floods and Paradise, California—a town of 26,000 that burnt to the ground, the fire killing 86 people.

It's a message many believe in, and Sanders delivered it by following the basic propaganda pattern. He described climate change as a global issue, then began to talk about its devastating local consequences. He introduced expert opinions, stating that scientists have said we have 12 years before the damage is no longer reparable. Sanders connected climate change with the deaths in Paradise and identified the fossil fuel companies as the devil *that receives too many tax subsidies.*

SANDERS' FINAL STATEMENT: "Under my administration, that would stop."

Regardless of your feelings on fossil fuels, climate change, or your political inclination, the point is that Sanders' presentation took a page right out of the propaganda playbook. He presented it as imminent, supported this with expert opinions, gave it a definitive time frame and described what the future would look like if we didn't act cohesively against this issue and vote for him: "Under my administration, that would stop."

Sanders's climate change position is unique to the concerns of our time, and his presentation followed the propaganda patterns, step by step.

By using the changing climate as a platform, he can evoke emotion to generate collective support. And by leveraging fear of an unlivable future, he can activate our survival instincts to conform and accept the opinions of others. Whatever we feel about climate change or politics, it's important to recognize this approach as manipulation of the masses in an effort to achieve a personal agenda.

Regardless of the issue or the cause, propaganda often uses our own beliefs in order to bypass our defenses by employing a set presentation structure.

Whether it's missile gaps or climate changes, illegal aliens or weapons of mass destruction, once you identify the patterns, you are free to examine the validity of the information and the costs of the solution offered.

"Beware the naked man who offers you the shirt off his back."

African Proverb

CHAPTER 19

SELLING YOUR TREASURE MAP

"PSSST BUDDY, WANNA BUY A TREASURE MAP?"

"No, thanks," you respond. "If it's a real map, why not dig up the treasure yourself?"

Your assessment: **Potential threat**.

But what if you overheard a group huddled in a corner whispering about their map to buried treasure? Interest piqued, would you strain to hear more?

Your assessment: **Potential reward.**

SAME MAP. Different reaction. Zero rationale. The point: Even though we may believe our reaction was logical, neither response was achieved by a rational evaluation of facts.

The response in both cases was formulated based on **feelings** about the information received—not rational assessment or logical reasoning. Again, emotion dictates our response while rationale takes the credit.

Good persuaders know that rationale has little to do with a successful presentation. They understand that emotion is at the core of an audience's reaction to whatever they're selling, be it cars or a war on terror. The more we believe rationale is leading our actions, the more our emotions can be leveraged to manipulate and control us.

Be it a negative headline, a politician preaching world-ending peril, or even a treasure-map salesman, professional persuaders have only to expose us to a possibility. From there, our evolutionary design ensures we assess the information for threat or reward, which dictates our actions and behavior.

Evolution has hardwired us with lineage-extending emotions that ensure we remain in a radar-like survival mode, continually processing everything, real or perceived, as either a threat or a reward.

Without these emotionally powered responses keeping us from harm's way and on constant lookout for reward, it's likely we wouldn't be here discussing what controls our behavior.

We may feel rational, but our emotions remain deeply embedded in the foundation of our decision process, our actions and behavior.

Professional persuaders know that the more rational a person believes they are, the less defense they will deem necessary to protect their emotions, and the more vulnerable they are to persuasion.

This is the primary (or rather, the primordial) element in the dark art of emotional manipulation.

Without emotion, trying to influence an audience is nearly impossible—unless you spend heavily on message repetition, an expensive strategy that leaves you defenseless when competitors present better features, buy more advertising, add a third scoop—or get emotionally relevant.

EMOTIONAL RELEVANCE

FROM CAVE ETCHINGS OF EPIC HUNTS TO FIRESIDE TALES of tribal struggles, we've evolved to pay attention to emotionally relevant communication.

As offside as this sounds, those charity advertisements featuring starving children from war-torn countries should have all of us reaching for tissue and our wallets, but they don't. Most of us are more impacted by ads featuring a playful puppy than a starving child.

The reason is based in how we process and decipher emotional relevance. Incoming messages that are too far removed from our own lives are dismissed, while those that resonate close to our emotional experience have incredible power to motivate.

When a message has emotional relevance, we instinctively search our own emotion vault to assess the message and empathize. Sadly, connecting emotionally with a playful puppy is within the range of most, while starving children are not.

When an offering is presented within the audience's range of emotional relevance, their motivation to respond is intensified. So whether it's employing inner beauty to sell soap, leveraging potential terrorist attacks to control a population, or using playful puppies to sell bathroom tissue, relevant emotion engages an audience's attention.

When an emotional message combines relevance, product and purpose, it becomes marketing rocket fuel, propelling an audience from attention to desire, connecting emotions to unemotional objects like shoes, cars and soft drinks.

EMOTIONALLY RELEVANT PRESENTATIONS can connect the audience to the product with an intensity that simply can't be achieved using rationale—unless functionality itself is transformed into an emotion.

EMOTIONAL FUNCTIONALITY

THROUGHOUT THE BOOK, I've revealed the true influencer in our decisions—and how emotion does the heavy lifting but rationale steps in to take the credit.

Early on, I mentioned that one of the dangers in this self-delusion is that we then try to persuade others while believing that rationale dictates decisions rather than emotion. Then, it gets messy.

Whether you're presenting treasure maps or Teslas, emotion outperforms, no matter what. And that brings me to some of the greatest emotional influencers on the planet, the marketing team at Tesla.

Tesla's journey to the center of the car world culture is driven by its ability not to present better functionality, but to attach function to an emotion.

As automotive luxury brands challenge Tesla for a share of the electric vehicle market, they would do well to understand that owners traded in their BMWs and Mercedes for new Teslas not because of eco-functionality, but because of the emotional reward the brand provides.

After all, if zero tailpipe emissions were the only motivator, then a Chevy Bolt would be a fine choice to reduce carbon footprints and ecological remorse.

What Tesla understands is that even though people passionately believe the protection of our planet is worthwhile, this belief is often unmatched by personal behavior. Meaning, people don't just buy an electric vehicle for its virtues.

Most of Tesla's competitors have thus far missed this point. Their early approach has centered on presenting zero emission functionality, believing this alone would influence their target audience of environmentally conscious consumers. It didn't.

When saving the planet failed to motivate, they tried educating consumers on other EV features, such as gas savings, low maintenance costs, speed, and smooth and quiet driving. Strike two.

From ads featuring families silently convening with nature, to polar bears hugging EV owners for their care of the planet, to presenting functionality as benefits—so far, for Tesla's competitors—it's been a marketing disaster.

According to *statista.com*, a leading research and analysis provider, Tesla accounted for almost 80 percent of all electric vehicles sold in the U.S. in 2019. (The closest competitor was Chevrolet, at seven percent.)

Tesla understands that connecting logically has low influence on behavior compared to connecting emotionally. It uses emotional connection of its product, design and even its functionality to deliver feelings of self-value and self-actualization, which follows Maslow's hierarchy of needs.

Sure, driving a Tesla is good for the environment. But that's not nearly as motivating as the effects of peer evaluation and social status. Buying a Tesla is emotional, owning a Tesla is rational and driving one is ecologically responsible. But Tesla has transcended the automobile, elevating its ownership into a lifestyle. Now potential new owners don't just hand over a preorder deposit (for a car that won't be delivered for months, or even years)—they make an emotional investment in the brand. It's not just an ecologically economical mode of transportation (that happens to generate intense horsepower and deliver ultra-luxury). It is a precisely crafted emotional experience, something other manufacturers would do well to embrace.

Combined with the current state of global connectivity, emotional relevance is critical to achieving effective communication. Understanding how it can be used to propel messaging will lead to the ultimate influence, social momentum.

OUR SOCIAL MOMENTUM

THE PHONE RINGS. It's my brother, calling to tell me about his stress-free existence. He lives eight hours away, yet we communicate in real-time while he walks the beach and I search for parking at Home Depot.

In the restaurant, a song plays in the background and I tap an app that identifies the tune and begin to add the artist to my playlists—until I feel my wife's eyes burning upon me, put the phone down and finish my anniversary speech.

Back home, my son asks a question that Albert Einstein would take time to ponder, but my thoughtful deliberation is cut short with, "Never mind, Dad, I'll just ask Siri." I feign disappointment but listen intently as the synthesized voice explains the unexplainable.

Connection to everything and everyone has rapidly moved from impossible to plausible to expected. Perhaps if I'd been born in the midst of this technical transformation, rather than well before it, the speed of change wouldn't be so alarming.

Yet my epoch offers perspective on how this **instantness** in everything from information retrieval to mobile connection has altered human development, and perhaps, where this momentum may take us.

But before we look at our evolutionary future, it's important we consider the history of our emotional connection. Or as Winston Churchill said, *"The farther back you can look, the farther forward you are likely to see."*

Our evolution was guided by a quest for survival, leading us to coexist in groups. It can be assumed that before language developed, prosperity within the tribe was related to how well our ancestors developed emotional insight and interacted.

Back then, our emotional evolution—knowing how to behave as trustworthy and recognizing those who weren't—was just as important to our survival as our genetic development.

Early on, we grew to recognize the safety in numbers, yet resource variability and the instability of migration limited a tribe's expansion.

This restricted population growth and more than likely impeded communication's progress until the invention of agriculture some 10,000 years ago. It is a subject Yuval Noah Harari explores in his book, *Sapiens: A Brief History of Humankind*, as he describes how the agricultural revolution introduced new ways to generate and predict food sources. With predictability came stability. This increased populations and initiated modern civilization, which brought about dramatic social and communication adjustments.

Fast-forward to the late 1700s and early 1800s, when the industrial revolution facilitated mass production. The need for workers resulted in populations moving off the farms and into the factories. Once again, society underwent immense adjustments in communication.

As the century progressed, new inventions such as the telegraph and telephone revolutionized accessibility, although most interaction remained person to person. Earlier instruments of mass communication such as the printing press were joined by radio, and then cinema and television.

Yet these tools remained largely under the control of a select few.

Early persuaders understood the power of influence these tools possessed and used them to control the masses.

Napoleon controlled the printing press; Hitler used the power of radio and film. In more recent times, similarly concentrated control of the media has pushed the political and personal agendas of the few onto the many. The start of the Spanish-American War is generally credited to two American newspaper owners who published exaggerated stories of atrocities to generate public and political support for the war, which in turn, supported their own personal and business interests.

THE MOMENTUM SHIFT

AS THE 21ST CENTURY ADVANCED, new technology was introduced, yet antiquated thinking still plagued opportunity. The Internet remained primarily a source of information storage and delivery. Even social media began as a file storage network.

It wasn't until 2003, when MySpace transitioned to social media, that we entered a new era. It would be another five years before interactive connection underwent its magnitude of change in our daily lives.

Facebook didn't reach 100 million users until 2008.

Now, according to Hootsuite, nearly 3.5 billion people are active on, or have access to, social media, with 3.26 billion instantaneously connected using mobile devices.

Online connection is growing by a million new users daily, and with mobile technology, we can expand our tribes and effortlessly connect beyond geographic boundaries. But it isn't just the opportunity to connect anywhere, anytime, that impacts our society. It is the ability to personally grow local stories into global obsessions. It is the opportunity to draw power from the few and put it into the hands of nearly half the earth's population (and growing).

It is this new capacity to captain our own platforms and create our own media that challenges the control of tyrants and the evolution of our communication abilities.

This new social momentum has created a culture of unrestricted interaction, impacting not only how we project our message, but also how we process and assess incoming information.

With more avenues of interaction comes greater volume, which has increased the pressure on our ability to process and evaluate the information received. This has greatly altered the way we respond.

Need an example? Send an email asking three unrelated questions. If you receive more than a single answer back, you are among a rarified few.

The ways we review, deliberate and assess value are under newly intensified pressure.

Now, any information failing to present instant emotional relevance is seldom responded to, pursued or shared. Plainly put, our allotted reaction time has been reduced to a mere thumb swipe.

Social momentum has elevated emotional relevance to hyper importance. Now, as the personal dictator of a communication's exposure, reach and delivery, if a message isn't immediately emotionally relevant to us or to someone else in our tribe, we simply move on.

EMOTIONAL MOMENTUM

THE PENDULUM HAS SWUNG BACK TO THE TRIBE—albeit a tribe of potentially thousands, millions or even billions. And like our primal ancestors whose prosperity depended on their emotional communication skills, once again, our influence depends on our ability to emotionally connect and communicate. Only now, with the advent of social interaction, emotional communication has far-reaching results.

Read and share news about "Das Auto" makers engineering false emission results and watch them pay billions in fines as "Das Executives" get chased from "Das Company." A tourist's photo of a homeless boy doing homework under the light of a McDonald's window becomes a global fundraiser. An ice water bucket-dumping ritual raises $115 million in less than a year. A mom posts a video of her seven-week-old son receiving hearing aids and reacting to her voice for the first time and it is watched more than 15 million times.

Emotion has always been at the core of effective communication. Now with communication barriers demolished, more avenues offering more access than ever before, the ability to influence has moved from the few to the many. Now anyone can influence everyone.

Today, our lives are dramatically different than those of our primitive ancestors, but our need to communicate effectively and influence others remains a top survival priority. Given this, it's reasonable to assume that our future prosperity will be dictated by our ability to emotionally persuade.

IT IS WITHIN THESE CHANGING CONDITIONS we find ourselves. The question is, how do we evolve to meet the challenges ahead?

With your new knowledge of the tactics and persuasive techniques of emotion's intense power, how will you use your new tools? Will you move towards manipulation? Or gravitate to persuasion and then go beyond to become influential?

Now that you understand these tools, how will you wield them? How will you evolve? As a manipulator, with small aims for personal gain? Or as an emotional revolutionary, with an unlimited capacity to make the world better as you improve your own life and reach?

"You have brains in your head. You have feet in your shoes. You can steer yourself any direction you choose."

Theodor Seuss Geisel, *Oh, the Places You'll Go!*

CHAPTER 20

THE EMOTIONAL REVOLUTION

IN EARLY 2014, ANNA CLARK, the founder of EarthPeople Media, wrote a fascinating article for the *Huffington Post* titled "How to Start a Revolution." In it, she wrote, "Revolutions are not always bloody rebellions." She described a revolution as **a disruptive catalyst … led by an idea … whose time has come.**

If we follow Clark's thinking and consider that nearly half the planet is now interacting and sharing what's personally relevant to them, social media's global connectivity is the **disruptive catalyst** that has redistributed the power of influence from the few to the many. The **leading idea whose time has come** is the transcending power of emotion.

In short, it's an emotional revolution. Or more precisely, the Emotional Re-evolution. And it is a costly movement to dismiss.

Before this emotional revolution collided with global interaction, consequences could be decided by those few with the power to manipulate the masses. But social momentum has radically changed the manipulator's base of power.

It is something some understand; others pay heavily for failing to evolve.

PRE-REVOLUTION, United Airlines could have physically dragged the concussed and bloodied passenger Dr. David Dao Duy Anh down the aisle, bashing his head, breaking his nose and teeth—because, hey, they needed his seat—and then covered up the incident with a little manipulative media cleansing.

But not **post-revolution**.

Cell phones captured the assault (or as United's CEO Oscar Munoz described it, *"passenger re-accommodation"*). Social momentum mixed with emotional relevance outran and outreached United's attempt at manipulating the consequences and presenting Dr. Dao as a "belligerent, disruptive passenger."

Because of emotion, the information spread faster on social media than it could be altered by the few who influence the many, United's communication team and their PR agency. The *Chicago Tribune* reported that the video posts of the episode were viewed 6.8 million times in less than a single day. It became a trending topic; most viewers called for a boycott. The incident, its handling and the widespread outrage prompted the airline's parent company to terminate Munoz's anticipated advancement to sit as the company's next chairman.

One Twitter user said it best: *"That must really hurt, losing a seat you expected to get."*

Munoz and United disregarded the emotional revolution. They relied on old tactics and paid heavily for it.

But not every company solves their predicament with pre-revolution attempts at mass manipulation. In 2008, Maple Leaf Foods faced a catastrophic listeriosis outbreak that caused deaths and illness.

Maple Leaf instituted a recall even before their product was officially linked to the outbreak. CEO Michael McCain used television, social media and YouTube to publicly acknowledge that he, his company and their product were to blame for the tragedy.

What makes them emotional revolutionaries is their immediate and authentic reaction. Even though it was considered by many to make the company vulnerable to legal action, McCain openly admitted that the tragedy had shaken consumer confidence in their company.

Later, he would tell the *Globe and Mail* during the crisis, "There are two advisers I've paid no attention to. The first are the lawyers, and the second are the accountants."

THE POWER OF THE EMOTIONAL REVOLUTION

HENRY FORD WAS DEFINITELY A REVOLUTIONARY, but perhaps not an emotional revolutionary. He made transportation affordable for the masses and let customers choose whatever color car they wanted—as long as it was black. With an emphasis on engineering functionality and price-point, Ford didn't embrace the power of emotion.

Chevrolet did. Despite starting years after Ford and being outsold nearly 30 to one in their first year, Chevrolet eventually surpassed Ford's sales. Chevrolet understood that choice is emotional, and emotion dictates decisions. It began offering its customers options. The question buyers faced was no longer, "What do you want to drive?" but "Who do you want to be?"

This art of using emotional persuasion isn't new. But the question is, if emotion can influence buyers to purchase one car brand over another—or convince iPhone owners to toss their perfectly good device into a drawer the minute the newest version is introduced—or alter voter opinion based on a candidate's trustworthiness (oxymoron?)—or persuade a nation to enthusiastically embrace war—then couldn't these emotional powers of persuasion also be harnessed to make the world a better place?

Couldn't these same techniques persuade people to use less plastic, exercise more, eat healthier, lower their carbon footprint and save for their future? If emotional persuasion can cause normal, caring and intelligent adults to fistfight over a doll, then couldn't it also be used to stop your aunt from smoking and convince people to buy only ethical brands? Or, if I was to stretch, even convince our delivery kid to throw the paper all the way onto our porch when it's raining? (Admittedly, some things may just be impossible.)

With the exception of our paper, the answer is yes. All we need is a little revolutionary thinking about persuasion, influence and, well, emotional manipulation.

At the beginning of this book, I asked that you give me a little leeway regarding the word **manipulation** and to look upon the word as an expression rather than hold tightly to its negative connotations.

Here, I'd like to ask you to consider emotional manipulation the same you would any other tool. Only this time, consider how it can be used in a revolutionary way to mold opinion, achieve great things and create win-win situations.

A FINAL WORD

DR. MARTIN LUTHER KING, JR. ONCE SAID, *"A genuine leader is not a searcher for consensus but a molder of consensus."*

How do I use manipulation to become an emotional revolutionary?

The first step in solving a challenge is understanding it. The deeper our understanding of the professional persuader's exploitive tactics, patterns and techniques, the better we become at identifying attempts to access our emotions and understanding how they influence our behavior.

Knowledge is a powerful defense against the persuader's Machiavellian maneuvers, but it also provides something else—an ability to use the dark art of emotional manipulation for the power of good.

But is there such a thing as good emotional manipulation? Can influencing the decisions of others actually be good rather than, say, malevolent? Simple answer—yes. It is the difference between manipulation purely for self-interest versus using emotional persuasion to improve your situation AND the situation of others around you. If it is win/win, then it's an emotional revolutionary act.

Over the years, many emotional revolutionaries emerged to achieve amazing things; most did it before the globe became interconnected. Some of my favorites include those who faced incredible adversity but enlisted emotional persuasion to get what they needed and achieve giant leaps in the greater good.

These emotional revolutionaries include Elizabeth Blackwell, the first woman to graduate from medical school, and the Polish scientist Marie Curie, the first female professor at the University of Paris and winner of the Nobel Prize. (Uh, twice.) I can't imagine Blackwell or Curie dealing with discrimination, hostility and the criticism against women in fields that were completely dominated by men without their deep understanding of emotional persuasion.

In high school, Bill Gates created his first computer program and convinced early investors of his version of the future. Steve Jobs, well-known for his persuasive tactics, lured the president of Pepsi, John Sculley, to join Apple by asking if he wanted to "sell sugar water for the rest of his life, or come with me and change the world?" Abraham Lincoln passed through Congress the 13th Amendment to the U.S. Constitution, permanently outlawing slavery, and Churchill persuaded the British Parliament against bending to Hitler's dictatorial powers. John F. Kennedy appealed to the nation's emotions with "Ask not what your country can do for you. Ask what you can do for your country."

Each of these world-changing individuals was or is an emotional revolutionary who, facing intense opposition, used emotion to manipulate and change public opinion, generate win-win results **and** achieve their own objectives.

The more you practice the skills demanded by the emotional revolution, the more you will experience profound changes and accomplishments in your life. At the same time, you will become expert at identifying and limiting the reach of those attempting to manipulate purely for self-serving purposes.

As an emotional revolutionary persuading for the purpose of good, you have the ability to influence, to impassion and to inspire others.

The power is in your hands.

A FINAL THOUGHT, OR TWO....

BUT FIRST, A SMALL TOKEN OF MY APPRECIATION.

Thank you for reading this book. I mean it. I know you could be doing something else, like walking the dog, washing a lamp, anything really.

As a thank you, I have written a new chapter and would like to give it to you. Just visit morrisonwrites.com/thankyou and you'll be whisked to the special bonus chapter. It may change the way you see the world.

Secondly, I'm constantly amazed at the feedback I receive from readers using persuasion to enrich the lives of others as emotional revolutionaries. So if you have thoughts on the book or something to share about how you improved your life and the lives of others, please send me an email at bill@morrisonwrites.com. I would love to hear from you and will absolutely respond.

PS: Until next time, thanks again for reading.

Sincerely,

Bill

If you are interested in more thoughts, insights and musings on the topic of persuasion, changing the audience's perception of your value, and other inspirational tidbits, head over to morrisonwrites.com.

REFERENCES AND RESOURCES

BOOKS

Ariely, Dan. *Predictably Irrational: the Hidden Forces That Shape Our Decisions.* Harper, 2010.

Bernays, Edward L. *Crystallizing Public Opinion.* Boni and Liveright, 1923.

Bernays, Edward L., and Mark Crispin Miller. *Propaganda.* Desert Books, 2018.

Bon, Gustave Le, and Charles Mackay. *Twin Classics of Crowd Psychology.* Traders Press, 1994. Includes *The Crowd: A Study of the Popular Mind*

Burns, James MacGregor. *Roosevelt: the Lion and the Fox.* Harcourt, 1956.

Brands, H. W. *Reagan: the Life.* Knopf, 2016.

Cialdin, R. B. *Influence: The Psychology of Persuasion.* HarperCollins, 2007.

Cleary, Thomas, and Sun Tzu. *The Art of War.* Shambhala, 1988.

Cuddy, Amy. *When They Trust You, They Hear You: A Modern Guide for Speaking to Any Audience.* Houghton Mifflan Harcourt, 2021. Expected in January 2021

Damasio, Antonio R. *The Feeling of What Happens: Body and Emotion in the Making of Consciousness.* Heinemann, 2000.

Dante, et al. *The Divine Comedy of Dante Alighieri ; Inferno.* Houghton Mifflin, 1886.

Darwin, Charles. *On the Origin of the Species. A Facsimile of the First Ed.* Harvard University Press, 1964.

Furedi, Frank. *Politics of Fear.* Continuum, 2006.

Gilbert, G. M. *Nuremberg Diary.* A Signet Book from New American Library, Times Mirror, 1961.

Gladwell, Malcolm. *Blink: the Power of Thinking without Thinking.* Back Bay Books, 2019.

Harari, Yuval Noah. *Sapiens: a Brief History of Humankind.* Harper Perennial, 2015.

Herman, Arthur. *Freedom's Forge: How American Business Produced Victory in World War II.* Random House Trade Paperbacks, 2013.

Hilter, Adolf. *Mein Kampf.* Hurst and Blackett, 1939.

King, Martin Luther. *Dream: the Words and Inspiration of Martin Luther King, Jr.* Blue Mountain Press, 2007.

Lieberman, Matthew D. *Social: Why Our Brains Are Wired to Connect*. Oxford University Press, 2015.

Maslow, Abraham. *The Hierarchy of Needs*. Institute of Management Foundation, 1998.

Nietzsche, Friedrich Wilhelm, and O. Levy. *Thus Spake Zarathustra*. Foulis, 1909.

Norman, Donald A. *Emotional Design: Why We Love (or Hate) Everyday Things*. Basic Books, 2005.

Packard, Vance Oakley., and Bill McKibben. *The Waste Makers*. Ig Pub., 2011.

Seuss, Dr. *Oh, the Places You'll Go!* HarperCollins Children's, 2011.

Watts, Alan. *The Book on the Taboo of Knowing Who You Are*. Vintage Books, 1989.

Whiting, Percy H. *The 5 Great Rules of Selling*. Dale Carnegie, 1978.

MOVIES AND FILM

12 Angry Men	1957	Orion-Nova Productions
A Few Good Men	1992	Columbia Pictures, etc.
Braveheart	1995	Icon Entertainment, etc.
Daddy's Home 2	2017	Paramount Pictures, etc.
Dead Poet's Society	1989	Touchstone Pictures, etc.
Mad Men (TV Series)	2007-2015	Lionsgate Pictures, etc. (AMC)
The Ghost and the Darkness	1996	Constellation Entertainment
The Shawshank Redemption	1994	Castle Rock Entertainment
The Power of Nightmares, The Rise of the Politics of Fear (Documentary Series)	2004	BBC

SPEECHES

President Franklin D. Roosevelt 1933 Inaugural Speech First inauguration of Franklin
D. Roosevelt - Wikipedia. https://en.wikipedia.org/wiki/The_only_thing_we_have_to_fear_is_fear_itself

President George W. Bush President's Remarks at the United Nations General Assembly
New York, New York September 12, 2002 doi: https://georgewbush-whitehouse.archives.gov/news/releases/2002/09/20020912-1.html

STUDIES

Ambady, Nalini, and Robert Rosenthal. "Thin Slices of Expressive Behavior as Predictors of Interpersonal Consequences: A Meta-Analysis." *Psychological Bulletin*, vol. 111, no. 2, 1992, pp. 256–274., doi:10.1037/0033-2909.111.2.256.

Campbell-Meiklejohn, Daniel K., et al. "How the Opinion of Others Affects Our Valuation of Objects." *Current Biology*, vol. 20, no. 13, 2010, pp. 1165–1170., doi:10.1016/j.cub.2010.04.055.

Carney, Dana R., et al. "What, When, and for How Long? Another Look at Judgmental Accuracy from Thin Slices of the Behavioral Stream." *PsycEXTRA Dataset*, 2004, doi:10.1037/e633912013-558.

Klucharev, Vasily, et al. "Brain Mechanisms of Persuasion: How 'Expert Power' Modulates Memory and Attitudes." *Social Cognitive and Affective Neuroscience*, vol. 3, no. 4, 2008, pp. 353–366., doi:10.1093/scan/nsn022.

Krishna, Aradhna, and Norbert Schwarz. "Sensory Marketing, Embodiment, and Grounded Cognition: A Review and Introduction." *Journal of Consumer Psychology*, vol. 24, no. 2, 2014, pp. 159–168., doi:10.1016/j.jcps.2013.12.006.

Miller, George A. "The Magical Number Seven, plus or Minus Two: Some Limits on Our Capacity for Processing Information." *Psychological Review*, vol. 63, no. 2, 1956, pp. 81–97., doi:10.1037/h0043158.

Prickett, Tricia J., et al. "First Impression Formation in a Job Interview: The Importance of the First 20 Seconds." *PsycEXTRA Dataset*, 2000, doi:10.1037/e413792005-571.

Schutz, William. "Fundamental Interpersonal Relations Orientation–Behavior Assessment." *PsycTESTS Dataset*, 1958, doi:10.1037/t02314-000.

MAGAZINE ARTICLES

Please Touch the Merchandise
Harvard Business Review by Lawrence Williams and Joshua Ackerman
on December 15, 2011

Why We Are Wired to Connect
Scientist Matthew Lieberman uncovers the neuroscience of human connections—
and the broad implications for how we live our lives
Scientific American, By Gareth Cook on October 22, 2013

How to Start a Revolution
02/26/2014 09:50 am ET Updated Apr 28, 2014
Huffington Post, By Anna M. Clark, the founder of EarthPeople Media

ACKNOWLEDGMENTS

AT 15, I VISITED RELATIVES IN EUROPE and returned with a pierced ear and a plan. I was going to live in London and become a writer.

My father said, "If you want to write, this is exactly what you are meant to do." (And, "Take out that f@&#ing earring.") He then left the room to call my uncle long distance.

At 22, after a few years of backpacking, I again expressed a desire to write. Dad eyed my earlobes and said, "If you want to write, this is exactly what you are meant to do."

Through the years, I'd hand Dad a new page or a half-written story, and each was discussed and deliberated upon. Each became the new fuel for his encouragement.

"This is exactly what you are meant to do."

Thank you, Dad. Even though you can't hold this one, or tell me, "This is exactly what you are meant to do", here it is, finished, published, printed.

And still no earring.

The closest thing to that familial support has come from my editor, Lori Bamber. Swift kicks of inspiration and gentle nudges of education in how to write the words people read. Thank you, Lori. Thank you.

Thank you, Megan Williams at TSPA, for your divine intervention and guidance in the publishing process. And for leading me to such fine people as Jazmin Welch, whose creativity delivered a cover, that, well, let's face it, is probably the reason you're reading the book.

I would also like to thank my brother Trevor for his input and friendship. Although he has become a cat person, no one should hold this against him.

Thank you, Tanya, Will and Finn, for riding along on this emotional rollercoaster and never, ever, mentioning that you didn't actually buy a ticket.

BILL MORRISON is a writer and consultant in the field of emotional positioning and consumer behavior. He has spent the last 25 years uncovering the elements of influence and persuasion that impact human motivation. After two decades of unprecedented success in condominium tower marketing, he now consults with corporations, brands and individuals on how to emotionally connect their audience with their offerings.

He lives with his wife and two sons on the West Coast of Canada, plays hockey with the same team he's been on for 30 years, and has a dog named Louie.

Manufactured by Amazon.ca
Bolton, ON

15084070R00162